# The Higher Dimensions
# Our Next Home

## A Spiritual View of
## The Twenty-first Century and Beyond

Also by Nancy Van Domelen

*Dreaming a New World —*
*A Spiritual Journey of Hope and Transformation*

# The Higher Dimensions
# Our Next Home

## A Spiritual View of
## The Twenty-first Century and Beyond

Nancy Van Domelen

Shining Mountain Publishing

Published by:
Shining Mountain Publishing
www.shiningmountain.net

Cover painting by Marika Popovits
Cover and book design by Vicki McVey
Author photo by Colleen Black

If you are unable to order this book from your local
bookseller, you may order directly from the publisher's website.

Library of Congress Catalog Number: 2005903513
ISBN: 0-9716106-1-4

Printed in the United States of America

First Edition

This book is dedicated to the people of Earth.
Like the ibex, the tough, hardy wild goat
that climbs to ever-higher ground,
humanity also perseveres
on its spiritual path to higher dimensions.

# CONTENTS

Acknowledgments . . . . . . . . . . . . . . . . . . . . . . . . . . . . . ix

Introduction . . . . . . . . . . . . . . . . . . . . . . . . . . . . . . 1

We Begin Again . . . . . . . . . . . . . . . . . . . . . . . . . . . . 5

Earth — a Laboratory for Soul Growth . . . . . . . . . . . . 13
Restoring Planetary Balance ◆ 16
Earth's Initiation ◆ 22
Three Steps in Earth's Healing ◆ 27
Why Natural Disasters ◆ 30
Earth's Role as a Living Library ◆ 34
A New Heaven and a New Earth ◆ 39

Cycles — Spiritual Patterns of Death and Rebirth . . . 43
The Unfolding Cycle of the United States ◆ 45

The Dance of Duality — from Conflict to Unity . . . . 53
The Law of Manifestation ◆ 58
National Initiation — a Crucible for Growth ◆ 61
The Play of Polarity ◆ 64
The War in Iraq — Spiritualization of the Human Heart ◆ 67
Duality—the Underlying Principle of Human Interaction ◆ 72
Bringing Duality into Unity ◆ 75

The Fourth Dimension — a Journey into the Now . . . 83
Guardians of the Flame ◆ 85
Emergence of a New Human Species ◆ 87
The Pathway to Higher Realms ◆ 89
Preparations for Fourth-Dimensional Travel ◆ 95
Fourth-Dimensional Reality ◆ 99
Multidimensional Consciousness ◆ 102

Developing Extrasensory Awareness ◆ 105
Time — the Ever-Present Now ◆ 108
Expanding Brain Capacity ◆ 110
The Many Dimensions of Heaven ◆ 111
Quantum Physics — a New Picture of Reality ◆ 115
Time's Shift into a New Paradigm ◆ 116

The Twenty-First Century and Beyond . . . . . . . . . . . 119
A New Age in Human Development ◆ 121
The Great Purification ◆ 124
The Secret of Eternal Life ◆ 126
Humanity's Spiritual Blueprint ◆ 127
Major Themes for the New Millennium ◆ 129
A Time of Awakening ◆ 131
The Gathering Storm ◆ 135
Earth Changes ◆ 137

Love — the Creative Force . . . . . . . . . . . . . . . . . . 149
Learning to Love Our Enemies ◆ 150
Learning to Love Ourselves ◆ 152
Functioning within a Larger Spiritual Context ◆ 154
The Primal Force ◆ 156
Developing a More Expansive View of Life ◆ 157

Definition of Terms . . . . . . . . . . . . . . . . . . . . . . . 162

Index . . . . . . . . . . . . . . . . . . . . . . . . . . . . . . . . . 165

# Acknowledgments

Many people have accompanied me during this creative endeavor. To all of them I would like to express my love and appreciation for their assistance. The following individuals deserve special recognition, since they provided significant contributions on behalf of this work:

Rebecca VanDenBerghe, who edited the transmissions with respect, always honoring the integrity of the message above all else;

Puja Parsons, who grounded each transmission energetically with a reverence for the connection between the realms of spirit and matter;

Sam Del Cielo, a caring friend whose encouragement and love for the information provided steady support and assistance during the birthing of the book;

Marika Popovits, whose painting graces the cover. Her artwork beautifully depicts the true essence of the book;

Jackie Karsky and Linda Del Cielo for their ongoing efforts to ensure that many have an opportunity to benefit from the spiritual message found in this book;

Cristin Hentges, who designed the signature of the group soul exactly as I have received it down through the years;

Sheila Dierks and the staff at WovenWord Press for their support, professionalism and skill in providing resources required for the publishing process;

My daughter, Jane Reagan, for her much needed computer assistance and my husband, Peter, for his extensive work in all areas of book production and distribution;

I want to express my love and thanks to every member of my family. They fill my life with joy.

# Introduction

As we begin a second book of transmissions from the realm of spirit, I would like to speak about the process that unfolded during the compilation of this work. What you are about to read was not conceived by me. I have served simply as a scribe or conduit, receiving information from a group soul that helps raise the vibrational frequency of individuals to a higher state of consciousness. My role was to quiet myself, attune through meditation and prayer, and then write whatever came to me in an altered state.

This unusual process started in the early years of the 1980's after the tragic death of my youngest son. The devastating loss turned me in an entirely new life direction – one that continues to this day. As a wife, mother and grandmother, I had served as teacher, educational administrator and community human service activist for many years. After my son's death, my frame of reference became more inward, and I began to explore the meaning of life within a broader spiritual context.

Throughout the last two decades, I received transmissions in the form of letters from the realm of spirit that contained loving wisdom and support for me in all areas of life. At first the contacts were from my son who had died, and finally they expanded to a group of souls who have become unseen friends and companions along the way. Over time, I came to value this unusual relationship with spirit as a significant part of my existence.

Years of personal contact passed, and then I was asked to receive transmissions that would be published for a broader human audience. After some serious soul-searching, I agreed. The first book is entitled *Dreaming a New World: a Spiritual Journey of Hope and Transformation*. The theme of this book is reflected in its title. Those on the realm of spirit ask us to see ourselves with clarity and truth, since only then can we start the process of creating a new and better world. In order to reach this point in human development, it is necessary that we look at all aspects of life from an expanded spiritual perspective. To assist in reaching this goal, *Dreaming a New World* offers a comprehensive look at the human condition – past, present and future.

Since many humans need to relate to a name, the group consciousness providing the information offered Lightbringers as a term of identification. They said that their purpose is to bring knowledge encoded within a specific vibrational frequency that emits light to any part of the universe activated in the unfolding of the Divine Plan. They indicated, however, that a better term for them is the symbol found throughout this book — half of a horizontal infinity sign with two intersecting lines. They say that it more accurately reflects their true essence.

When I began the transmission process for this second book, I quickly found myself in uncharted waters. Information regarding the fourth dimension began to come through offering a vivid picture of life I knew nothing about. It required a leap of faith, plus the honor and love I had developed over time for my friends in spirit, to continue the process and stay the course.

As I received more transmissions, I began to notice they contained a rhythm and cadence that had a melodic vibrational quality. Words, phrases and ideas seem to weave themselves into the very fabric of the book, appearing and then reappearing like the refrains of a symphony. When I inquired about this difference in presentation, I was told that the second book mirrors the essence of the fourth dimension, where everything exists in its totality, reflecting and refracting the nature of the Divine Creator over and over again.

Whereas *Dreaming a New World* provided spiritual concepts relating to everyday life, this new material seemed to be more abstract and less oriented to the world of matter. I questioned whether people would be interested in multidimensional consciousness. The response from spirit was for me to continue with trust and faith knowing that all was in divine order. It was almost as if I received a loving embrace that reassured me there was far more to the world unfolding about me than I could ever envision.

As time passed, to my surprise I found many people expressing interest in the higher dimensions. There seems to be a spiritual awakening occurring worldwide as the inhabitants of Earth struggle to deal with the conflict and violence surfacing throughout the planet. Many want to find a more loving path as an alternative to the acts of warfare escalating in our world. And so I offer some gentle words from the realm of spirit. May they be uplifting and bring peace and understanding to all who connect with this source!

Nancy Van Domelen
2005

# We Begin Again

We welcome you, our dear Earth friends. Let us begin again our ongoing discussions regarding the nature of reality. With these words, we embark upon our second series of transmissions from the realm of spirit. In our first book, *Dreaming a New World,* we presented a wide variety of topics for our readers' consideration offered from a spiritual perspective. We took a journey through time, past, present and future, placing special emphasis on the key issues currently facing human beings on planet Earth – love, death, relationships, sexuality, healing and addictions, to name a few.

We spoke about how to develop personal power and recognize the ebb and flow of energy all about us. We brought information to our readers concerning the appearance of a new human species with greatly expanded capabilities and described in detail the great awakening that humanity is experiencing.

We gave a preview of the world to come, which will bring a new Earth peopled by beings very different from those currently inhabiting the planet. Tremendous transformation is occurring, and a more advanced order of humanity is about to emerge. In order for this to happen, we asked the people of Earth to begin expanding their view of themselves and the reality of the world in which they live.

It is at this point that we offer a second book devoted to the expansion of human consciousness. These works combine an unusual partnership – one that involves the mutual cooperation of a human receiver and scribe on the Earth plane interacting with our group soul on the realm of spirit. Our relationship with the author of this book has existed for over twenty years. A strengthened and solidified bond of trust has made the creation of our work together possible.

We would like to expand upon who we are and how we function in the many universes of time and space. We are a group soul or spiritual construct. We possess many facets that reflect the essence of the Almighty. We retain individuality within a group consciousness that continually carries out its purpose within the Plan of the Creator.

We know that it may be difficult for our readers to understand and relate to the concept of a group consciousness that functions with the participation of individual souls. The primary reason for this difficulty is that each soul on the Earth plane, at the present time, operates with a sense of separation from other humans, the Earth, and the Creator of All That Is. The idea of living within a matrix of other beings that function as a unified whole is totally foreign and incomprehensible to most people on your planet.

However, this lack of awareness is slowly shifting, as the Earth moves into the heart of the Milky Way Galaxy. Here the strongest centrifugal powers within your universe create the spiritual force needed for the human evolutionary process. This center of your beautiful galaxy is a powerful womb of intense vibratory energy that breaks down and creates anew the varying human experiences leading to soul growth and development.

We are aware that few beings on your planet think in galactic terms. But this will change very soon. When Earth emerges from this area of your galaxy in another twenty years, it will be totally transformed. Higher vibratory frequencies will infuse light-encoded molecules onto the planet, illuminating everything that lives with an increased level of consciousness.

When this occurs, many will lift their heads, open their eyes and stretch as if awakening from a long, deep sleep. To their amazement, they will see fine gossamer threads extending from themselves to every thing about them. They will realize, for the first time in many eons, that they truly are connected to all that exists in their world. This realization will catapult humanity into galactic participation as citizens of a wide, diverse world of many differing forms of manifestation.

Can you grasp the enormity of this transformation? When humans know that they are part of a collective energy field that includes all that exists about them, the view that people have of each other and their world will change completely. You will be participating in a new and wondrous time — one anticipated for centuries by the more advanced souls on Earth.

Our readers may be asking that we further identify ourselves. In our first book, we provided the name of Lightbringers to describe ourselves since our primary function is to bring information for illumination and enlightenment. Humans have given us many different names down through time as they attempted to incorporate our essence into third-dimensional reality. The best term that can be used to describe us is the symbol found at the beginning of this chapter – half of a horizontal infinity symbol crossed by two lines. Any other designation is incomplete. The use of this symbol throughout this book will help many readers remember its significance to them at other times in their lives.

We would like to provide a brief overview of this second series of transmissions. Three fundamental ideas are presented in seven chapters. These numbers have great significance spiritually. The number *three* expresses the triune nature of the Creator, the highest expression of life in the universe. Energy that manifests within a triangular field is the most harmonious and enduring for those living on Earth. It will soon be recognized that for any creative act to be successful, it must come from a base of three. The number seven has long epitomized the combination of triune spirit joining with the four-fold foundation of physical matter.

Why is this book formed on the structure of the numbers three and seven? We have created for our readers a vibrational forcefield that will contain as great a significance to the reader as the book itself. While your minds receive the verbal content, your bodies will be experiencing the energy field connected to this work. For many, a mental and spiritual expansion will occur that will lead to a shift in other areas of human expression. Are you ready and willing for this change to happen?

You will find that the book contains recurring themes. They are intended for emphasis and serve as a unifying principle for the message we bring. Concepts are presented with a cadence and rhythm that flows in a stream of consciousness akin to a river circling and then returning to a location previously passed. Ideas will appear and reappear like a refrain offering a glimpse of the expanded awareness incarnating souls on Earth are developing on their spiritual journey back to reunion with the Creator.

You will find us using many different names in these transmissions to identify God. We do this for a specific reason. Once a name for God and a definitive practice are established, the human propensity for formalization and crystallization comes into being. Control mechanisms are set in motion, preventing the ability to connect directly with our Divine Source. Down through the ages, much suffering has been caused by those who have tried to force others into rigid religious rituals and practices, one of them being a mandatory name for God.

This book will offer three primary areas for consideration. The first contains a view of the condition of the Earth – physically, emotionally and spiritually. There is a need for inhabitants of your planet to connect with and love the great being that sustains your physical existence and see her in an entirely different way. We shall attempt to provide that new perspective to our readers as we look at the Earth's cycles, her process of initiation, and role as a living library within the galaxy. Finally we shall consider the importance of restoring planetary balance in this first century of the new millennium.

The second theme of this book will speak to the ever-increasing clouds of warfare that are spreading throughout the globe. Powerful physical, social, and political forces are coalescing with greater intensity. In order that you may understand what is transpiring, we shall acquaint our readers with the underlying dynamic of your universe — duality. Unity is the positive solution to conflict and can only be found by transcending duality and polarity. We shall look in depth at the twenty-first century and beyond as we explore the ultimate goal — love for the Earth, its inhabitants, and the Divine Creator of All That Is. As the people of Earth learn to attune directly to their soul wisdom, the dark energies spawning hurtful actions toward others will dissipate and be removed from your planet.

Finally, we will offer a description of the higher realms of existence to be found above that of the third dimension. In the next one thousand years, Earth's inhabitants will increase their abilities to access higher dimensions of time and space, starting with travel into the fourth dimension, the Eternal Now. One of the most important experiences that the incarnating soul can have is to move upward on the spiral of the Creator, growing in knowledge and wisdom. As the soul does so, it will encounter beings and realms, which will offer new challenges for growth.

Many humans on your planet are going to take a great step forward in the next twenty years. They will start to go to these higher dimensions through astral travel and soul journeys. By doing this, they will gradually become aware that they are multi-dimensional beings with powers far beyond what they currently realize. In this book, we will attempt to provide a road map for the journeys ahead and describe some of what will be encountered.

We will speak to the preparations that will be required of those who are going to undertake this expansion in consciousness. There are practices of physical, mental, and spiritual disciplines that will be necessary for those who have committed themselves to be progenitors of a new human species. The prototype for this species is being formed and developed from the humus of those human beings who currently reside on the planet.

Earth's incarnating souls need to recognize their greater role, which they agreed to hold during this time, and honor it in all ways. They also need to know in concrete, practical terms what they can do personally to participate in the birthing of this new prototype of human being. We shall provide this information for their consideration and enlightenment. The twenty-first century will set the tone for these extraordinary events. Are we all not fortunate to be living in such a wondrous time? Let us begin.

# Earth – A Laboratory for Soul Growth

In the earliest days, the beings residing on the etheric plane surrounding the Earth were aware that this area of the galaxy was established for a specific purpose. At that time, the physical condition of the Earth was very different. There was a dense atmospheric cloud surrounding the planet, blocking the direct rays of the sun. Much of the Earth was water, with one giant landmass located in the central and southern portion of the planet.

Lush plants grew to an enormous size and were the only form of life. The fertility of the new land and the amount of readily available water provided continuous sustenance for an unbelievable array of luxuriant plant growth. The abundance of the plant and mineral kingdom was an essential foundation for the complex life forms that would later appear. This long period of flora and fauna provided a nurturing matrix for the creation of the new thinking race.

Human life emerged when the evolution of the planet was deemed ready. Much has been written about how this process occurred. Some of it has been accurate, and some has not. The key quest has been for the so-called missing link between hominid life and intelligent, modern humanity. The search will never reveal this link because it never existed. Early sub-human life appeared as a natural outgrowth of primitive mammalian evolution, but the spark of spirit was very dim in these early humanoid forms.

It was then determined by the divine creative powers of the universe that the time had come to introduce intelligent life onto the Earth. Beings from other star systems were enlisted to assist in the birth of this more advanced species. They provided the DNA that was the basis for the human prototype about to begin its long sojourn upon the planet. Earth was a verdant paradise, a welcoming womb for the appearance of animal and human life. Much spiritual direction was given from the various realms that were responsible for the preparation of this planet. The richness of the physical environment was an essential ingredient needed for the high level of development that was to occur here.

Earth is the place where the worlds of spirit and matter are meant to meet and fuse. From this union will appear the spiritualized human being, a true child of universal consciousness who will play and create throughout the many worlds of Divine Oneness. Before this cosmic dance could begin, the long road of human development had to be traveled with all of its joy and pain. Once that journey is completed, those living on this plane will become realized beings – true co-creators with All That Is. Do you not think that the long road is well worth the final destination?

We now ask the inhabitants of Earth to raise your heads, look around you, and connect with the long-forgotten knowledge that you are citizens of the universe who came to your beautiful planet to take part in a divine experiment. You were selected because of the great power and beauty you possessed. In the many eons that have passed since you arrived, you have forgotten the truth of who you are. Now you must remember and activate the divine part of yourselves that has lain dormant for so long.

Important work is afoot. Earth is completing a twenty-six-thousand-year cycle. During this extended period, many great cultures have risen, flourished, and then disappeared into oblivion, leaving permanent traces in the genetic code and subconscious memories of those who have resided here down through the eons. For example, the knowledge of the ancient civilizations of Atlantis and Lemuria is encoded in the subconscious memory banks of all human beings presently living on your planet.

As more and more people start to connect to their spiritual roots, the recognition of the key role that these two cultures played over thousands of years will come into prominence. When that time arrives, there will be actual discoveries to prove what everyone has known subconsciously all along. The single most important element of these discoveries will be the awareness that you have access to everything that has ever happened to you though the avenue of your subconscious data banks. That awareness will be a giant step forward for humankind. Outer physical validation will no longer be necessary for humans to know about the past from whence they came.

Therefore, we ask that all readers of these words reflect and show new interest in the vast significance of the subconscious mind. Introductory work has occurred in the past century or more regarding the role of the subconscious mind as part of the psychological nature of the human race. However, the subconscious mind is a much more extensive reservoir of vital information than is understood at the present time. The ability to access formative experiences from another time frame will expand the physical brain and personal human awareness exponentially.

## Restoring Planetary Balance

The world about you is going through a process of extreme change. Climate is being impacted and changed in cycles of ever increasing severity. Weather patterns are being altered, with unusual conditions becoming the norm in almost all areas of the Earth. The intensity of the sun's rays is now a major concern to human beings, with drought and scarcity of water a familiar phenomenon. Warming at the poles resulting in rising seashore levels throughout the Earth is creating an instability in the planet's rotational course.

People are becoming more aware of the danger of planetary disruption on a worldwide scale. By the year 2015, the enormity of the problem will be much more evident. We ask that the readers of these words attend to our message regarding this situation. All of these seemingly negative events have a truly positive outcome in the overall scheme of things.

The Earth is experiencing a major catharsis meant to bring cleansing and purification on all levels. Periodically, and in an inherent rhythm, the Earth renews itself through what would appear to be catastrophic means. For those humans living on the planet during one of these periods, it would seem that the Earth is acting in a cruel and capricious way since many people lose their homes and lives. But at a higher level, all those participating in the great changes recognize what a beautiful process it actually is.

Most beings know at a deep soul level that they are facilitating the transformation that is taking place when they attune to the vibratory wavelengths that are invoking the changes. As they connect to the energy emanating from within the Earth, they become conscious co-creators with their mother planet in a powerfully direct way.

You may ask, "How does this connection occur in practical, concrete terms?" As human beings raise their vibratory wavelength through meditation and other means of attuning to higher energy sources, they increase their electromagnetic forcefield. This increase in vibratory power creates a beacon that pulsates with a projecting rhythm, sending healing energy into the Earth's atmosphere.

Those individuals who feel deeply the vibratory patterns of the Earth can be of great assistance in the coming years. They can soothe and soften the impact of destructive energies, which will be intensifying in the years ahead. This helpful process can be done in a number of ways. We will indicate what some of the more significant activities are.

Each time you meditate, we ask that you set aside a short time to express love and appreciation to the Earth. Visualize a healing green ray coming from the third eye in the middle of the forehead and moving out in expanding concentric circles until the entire planet is enveloped in a cloud of light. In times of destructive weather patterns, gather with others to chant, meditate and project healing energy to the affected geographic areas.

Dancing and drumming, as done all over the Earth by indigenous peoples, have long been a means of restoring balance to the planet. We ask that these practices continue and increase since they possess enormous healing energies for all beings residing in your dimension. But the most significant help humans can give the struggling planet is to see her as a living, nurturing being offering a support system to all who reside within her sphere.

As this awareness grows, humans will significantly alter all decisions, which adversely affect the planet. They will grow more protective of their mother, the Earth, and will stop those activities that bring harm to the physical environment. As this happens, human degradation of the planet will lessen. Severe weather conditions will moderate, restoring peace and serenity at all levels.

However, we do not want to imply that this will occur rapidly. A significant portion of those living on Earth needs to evolve into a new level of consciousness. This change has begun and is growing, but much more expansion of human awareness has to occur before a reversal of current conditions can take place. So we ask you who read these words to commit yourselves to entering the vanguard of those who want to love and heal the Earth. It is one of the most important things that anyone can do at this point in time.

Another way to restore planetary balance can be found in an area seldom considered by those living on the Earth plane. It consists of communing with spirit in the hours just before dawn. At the end of the day, the spiritual energies start to accumulate and increase throughout the dark of the night. Because of this phenomenon, it has always been recognized as auspicious to set aside a time within this period to open up to the realm of spirit. Monks, nuns, and others who have taken vows within a religious order commonly pray and meditate in the middle of the night. They have known that the spiritual energies are the most powerful during these hours.

Why is this so? The answer is very simple. The Earth exists on a plane of duality or opposites. Whenever the forces of light are the most prominent, there is an attraction for the forces of darkness. Correspondingly, when darkness is predominant, the vibratory powers of light are activated to establish balance. You ask then why does it not become light during the nighttime hours? It is because the law of duality keeps the light forces in check so as to honor the natural laws of this realm.

What is important to remember here is that the vibratory energies of light are very close during the dark of the night. In these hours, major connections can be made to the realm of spirit if one is awake, quiets the mind and enters into a receptive state. At the present time, the frantic pace of life and the barrage from the energies of modern technology cause many individuals to have problems sleeping. All kinds of medications have come into existence to assist one in getting to sleep.

The irony in this situation is that what the individual really needs is to be awake and attentive to the realm of spirit, which is close and available. Sleep is not what the person requires. Since the western world has moved so deeply into materialistic ways, there is no period set-aside during the day to stop and prayerfully honor the Divine Creator. Because this act is a basic human need, the spirit within interrupts nighttime sleep so that the person can attune to the higher realms during the peace and quiet of these hours.

Therefore, we ask those of you who awaken in the night or cannot sleep to look at what is happening with a very different view. Recognize your human need for connection to the creative forces of the universe. Quiet yourselves and sink into deep communion with the Divine Creator in whatever manner is appropriate to your belief system. Use slow, rhythmic breathing as your method of entering a prayerful state. Then just be, floating in the arms of Universal Love.

The amount of sleep that you miss will be offset by the higher vibratory energies entering and radiating throughout your body. You will awaken in the morning refreshed and energized — ready for the day in a far better fashion than if you took a sleeping pill. Sleeplessness is a modern problem of astounding proportions. It is no more than a reflection of the lack of meaningful time during the day to perform a basic human act — that of attuning to and honoring the source of our existence.

So, we ask that you attend to our words and trust the import of what we say. Try our suggestion. You have nothing to lose and everything to gain. What a different place the Earth would be if everyone worldwide would set aside time in a twenty-four hour period to connect with the realm of spirit, directly and with intent. Visualize the energy of vibratory light that would encircle the planet, healing and uplifting all those who live on this plane! We would have a new Heaven and a new Earth, would we not? And, secondarily, we would solve our sleeping problems within the wink of an eye.

We repeat that this time in which you live on the Earth plane is one of great change, transformation and wonder. To those presently living on your planet, our words may seem to be off the mark in some respects. Everyone recognizes the rapidity with which life is changing at all levels of existence, but few see transformation or wonder in the events that are occurring daily throughout the world. In fact, it appears to most people that society and culture are disintegrating in almost every area of life.

And there is truth in this perception, for a twenty-six-thousand-year cycle is coming to a close. Any cycle, particularly one of such great duration, brings to the surface elements of the life experience that are not to be carried over into the emerging age. There are two basic reasons for this release. First, certain life lessons are considered mastered and do not need to be repeated. Secondly, the negative aspects of certain conditions must be relinquished so that they cannot affect adversely the newly forming higher cycle of experience.

Today's extensive release of negative energy in all areas of life appears painful and destructive to the casual observer. It is difficult to see the elements of rebirth and transformation as the Old World ends and a new one is created. And it certainly does not seem that there is anything wonderful about the wars, violence, suffering, and death that exist on many continents throughout the planet. However, if one looks from the higher plane of spiritual understanding, it is possible to see the unfolding perfection in this human journey up the spiral of life.

When a mother gives birth to her unborn child, the process is painful indeed. All her energies are focused on bringing this new being into the world. The entire inner structure that has supported the child during nine months of gestation in the mother's womb is being abandoned. It has served its purpose and will not be taken with the new being into the life that waits. It is widely recognized, however, that this act of leaving the support and nurturance of the mother's body is traumatic and hurtful in many ways.

We would never suggest that the newly born child should hold on to the placenta and afterbirth and bring them along to be used in the life ahead. On the contrary, the old support system is discarded. And so it is with the Old World, which is in its death throes today. No longer is it needed to provide the matrix for life expression. There is a profound transformation occurring throughout the Earth. Out of the ashes of the old is arising a new age. This process of moving up onto a higher spiral of life is incredible indeed. If one could consciously realize that every painful event or act is ultimately contributing to a new and better world, it would be possible to experience fully the wonder of this great time.

# Earth's Initiation

There is much to be revealed about the coming twenty-first century. The times facing the inhabitants of Earth are going to be remarkable indeed. Much will change in the next ten decades. Soon a new cycle will begin, closing out the previous age that has been in effect for thousands of years.

In the past, those who had access to the ancient wisdom waited patiently for this new age on your planet to begin. They knew that in the far distant future the entire planet and its inhabitants would take a quantum leap forward. They also knew that the majority of humans coming to the Earth in the future would function within a matrix that would support a higher level of consciousness. They continually prepared for the great initiation that the planet would undergo in the coming millennium.

The idea of a planet experiencing an initiation may seem strange. This is so only if one is unaware that everything that exists possesses a spirit connected to the Divine Source. The Great Spirit inhabiting the Earth is mighty indeed. This being is feminine in nature and manifestation, which is why the Earth is primarily land and water. Of the four primary elements, these are the two containing the feminine essence energetically.

All of the major activities on the Earth's surface originate out of a feminine construct. New cultures and mighty nations are birthed repeatedly down through the ages to provide a framework for the spiritual development of incoming souls. There is much activity in the physical creation of communities, which will provide homes to those entering this plane. Education, building, commerce, agriculture and religion were important elements of the great cultures existing in the past and continue to be so at the present time.

This feminine overlay of life on the planet emanates from the soul inhabiting the Earth. She is currently called Gaia by many. This great being agreed to nurture and support everything that lives on her surface. She also knew that as humanity progressed, she would have to grow in consciousness in order to provide the planetary sustenance needed by all of her children. This spiritual process is called initiation, since it involves expansion brought about by arduous work in order to rise to a higher level.

Initiation is generally an agonizing process that involves the death of the old form, followed by transformation into a more elevated state of awareness and functioning. In one sense, the beautiful entity sustaining the Earth is dying so that she can attain a higher level of consciousness to support the new species of human being that is emerging at this time. The violent climatic conditions of floods, earthquakes, droughts, storms and volcanic eruptions are the physical indicators of her great travail.

Presently, there is apprehension, doubt and fear amongst many of the inhabitants of Earth regarding these physical manifestations. If there were the understanding, however, of what is happening, an entirely different attitude towards these events would prevail. People all over the globe could help their Earth Mother by remaining calm and trusting about the outcome of disturbing climatic occurrences. They also could send energy and encouragement to her through individual and group rituals designed to heal and uplift.

What we are asking is of utmost importance! For the people of Earth to see themselves as spiritual beings who inhabit a planet that also has soul consciousness is an enormous step upward on the spiral of life. When humanity relates to this great being through direct interaction, soul to soul, a harmony of transcendent beauty will engulf the planet, raising the vibration of all residing on her surface. Then a new Earth will appear in the heavens ready to take her rightful place as an abode of peace and love, welcoming all those wishing to live within her vibratory field.

This twenty-first century carries within its essence the vibration of the number three. This vibration creates harmony and balance in any given situation where it is manifesting. Generally, when one thinks of harmony and balance, there is an immediate association with the idea of peace. However, it would be inaccurate to think that this century will be one of peaceful tranquillity and love. As it unfolds, it will be evident that the opposite is true. In order to achieve this goal, it will be necessary to face the negative forces that are preventing balance from occurring. The Earth must go through a process of transformation in order to support humanity's move up the spiral of life.

This change is a form of initiation. The great soul inhabiting your planet must ascend to a higher vibrational level. She knows full well that a new, more advanced species is coming and that she must help prepare the ground upon which these new beings will walk. An initiation is a process of metamorphosis resulting in a higher level of consciousness. It is achieved through intense work and inner travail. The soul of your planet has agreed to embark upon this spiritual task so that she can continue to nurture the life she sustains.

This initiatory process will directly impact all that lives on the Earth, especially human beings incarnating in this time frame. There will be turmoil – physically, emotionally, psychologically and spiritually from pole to pole. When the smoke clears, a true state of balance will form the matrix for the new age that is waiting to be born. Then people all over the Earth will recognize that in order to reach a state of positive equilibrium, it is necessary to confront what is hindering it from manifesting.

The physical portion of the Earth's initiation will focus on the very degradation of the planet itself, brought about by the unbridled technological development of the industrial nations of the West. The Earth is responding to the actions that are impeding the flow of her life force. Increasingly violent climatic conditions are becoming commonplace occurrences all over the globe and will escalate in the coming years.

The Earth is responding to the manner in which she is being abused. Only when humans learn again to revere the Great Mother that sustains all life will physical balance manifest. Technology unleashed without spiritual awareness must become a thing of the past. If it is allowed to continue unchecked, it will poison the ground upon which you walk.

No longer will the air you breathe sustain you; nor will the atmosphere protect you. Human beings are the custodians of the planet. You must demonstrate a mature responsibility to this task with which you have been entrusted. Then, and only then, will the blessed planet that supports you reach that state of harmony and balance needed to birth a new and better time for all.

We have said that the Earth will be experiencing an initiation on many levels – physical, emotional, psychological and spiritual. The reader of these words may be wondering how a planet can have an indwelling spirit that experiences an emotional initiation. What exactly do we mean here, and how will this phenomenon manifest? We shall try to express as clearly as possible the concept of emotional initiation by a planet. In metaphysical thought, the emotions are ruled by the element of water. Emotions are held in the astral plane, which surrounds the Earth on an unseen energetic level. When a planet goes through death and rebirth, the astral plane with its accompanying emotional overlay is impacted severely.

Every place where water is found on Earth, in oceans, lakes, rivers, ponds, streams, and the very atmosphere itself, will experience a catharsis and upheaval of major proportions. Let us look first at the astral level surrounding your globe. In the most ancient representations of the Earth, it was depicted as an ovoid shape with many concentric layers encircling it, both within the planet and projecting out beyond its solid shape in ever finer layers of essence.

All emotions felt by the inhabitants of Earth down through time are collected and held at this astral level as part of the record of human evolution on your planet. These emotions run the gamut from the most positive and loving to the most negative and hurtful. They form the record of all human emotional experience on Earth. In one respect they are similar to a human being's subconscious mind, which serves as a repository of past experiences generally unrecognized at the conscious level.

It is important for souls living on Earth to awaken and remember that the mother sustaining them possesses emotions just as they do. Also, this great being carries within her essence all the feelings every person has experienced in the past and will have in the future. Do you not have a responsibility to maintain positive, loving emotions so that your individual contribution to the astral plane will be beneficial and not harmful to the Earth and all of her inhabitants?

As the Earth goes through an astral level initiation, there will be first a purging and then a cleansing and healing. The purging has started and is in full sway now. This is why there has been so much anger, hatred, and warfare throughout the twentieth century. Much of it is caused by very ancient emotions being released from the Earth's astral plane and coming directly into the vibratory field of everyone living in this age. At the same time, a great awakening is underway. It is growing stronger, reflecting the efforts of humans to raise the spiritual vibration that has accumulated from those who have incarnated on Earth down through the eons.

And so these emotional dualities exist in your daily lives, impacting you in countless ways. It is for this reason that we continually urge you to balance and center yourselves through meditation, attunement to nature and spiritual practices. They will help you weather the great emotional cleansing now in process and will contribute to the healing of humanity and the Earth itself.

## Three Steps in Earth's Healing

There are three steps in this process of emotional initiation. The first is an extensive purging of the negative emotional energy that has collected for eons on the astral plane surrounding the Earth. At periodic intervals, this type of release happens in order to bring forth a higher level of experience for those who are coming into incarnation.

The time of purging is most difficult for those living upon the surface of the Earth. All the destructive emotions of hate, anger, greed, and lust are being released from the astral level and are entering the physical realm, impacting every life form. The twentieth century was the time of greatest release, and all areas of life on Earth reflected it.

In this one-hundred-year period, continuous and destructive wars throughout the globe unleashed the furies of hate and anger. As individual and corporate wealth increased worldwide, greed became the order of the day, with the welfare of the people assuming secondary importance. Sexuality reached a level of license and permissiveness, reflecting in a short, intense span of time the lustful actions of humans down through the centuries.

If the inhabitants of the Earth had known at a conscious level that the horrors of the current period were ultimately beneficial in nature, it would have been easier to ride out the storms and travail of these times. In order for the planet and the life residing on her surface to move to a higher level of consciousness, the emotional cancers of the past have to be eradicated. And so it was that ancient evils were released onto all levels of life for cleansing and healing.

The children of Earth are approaching the conclusion of this first step. The second step of cleansing is starting to manifest on the astral level. This purification is reflected in the rising spirituality found in people and in their actions throughout the globe. The emotional wounding and pain of the past is being cleared away by the loving behavior of all those attempting to help. Every time a person performs an act of kindness or tries to bring peace into any inflamed situation, a cleansing of old emotional trauma occurs.

The third step of emotional healing will happen as incarnating souls insist that peace and love be the guiding principle in human affairs. When a certain number of people regularly perform the spiritual practices of prayer, meditation and attunement to the Creative Force, the critical mass will be reached; and a shift of major proportions will begin. The Earth's emotional transformation will be complete. A new and better world will then appear, ready to support the emerging species that awaits entry.

In every way, this time is one of much needed cleansing and growth for the planet and all those currently residing upon it. The astral realm is the first higher plane to interact with and penetrate the spiritual space of human beings. It contains all the emotions that constantly interweave with the human nature of those residing on this planet. It provides the color, the beauty and the intense feelings that accompany the human condition.

Every emotion felt by humans is released and reflected on the astral realm, where it is kept in memory, just as your computers retain data and information. These emotions, no matter how uplifting or negative, are contained within an astral storage bank located on a plane that links all life throughout the Earth's planetary system. At periodic intervals, higher spiritual forces cleanse and purify the Earth's vibratory atmosphere to orchestrate a needed release and to provide planetary balance and harmony. This is what is occurring at the present time.

Just think about this concept for a moment. Many of you reading this book are devoted environmentalists. Did it ever occur to you that you are polluting the very environment you love and want to protect by your negative expression of emotion? For this is truly the case. The astral level connects with weather and climatic changes occurring on the surface of the Earth, causing damaging rain, drought, earthquakes and volcanic activity. It is now time for the souls in incarnation to take responsibility and be accountable for their part in creating the destructive weather existing all over the planet.

The release of this emotional astral energy is necessary now, since the Earth is moving to a higher frequency and needs to clean the astral level of all negative emotion so that it will not be passed on to the new age that is waiting to be birthed. Every individual currently residing on the Earth must undertake the task of thoroughly and honestly facing any darkness held within his or her emotional nature and remove it from expression. If anger, fear, grief, or any other negative emotion starts to surface, one must acknowledge its presence, release it, and rise to a higher expression of that emotion. For anger, there would be peace and harmony; for fear, courage and trust; for grief, acceptance and love. This is the true meaning of alchemical change – the transforming of a baser condition to a higher expression.

## Why Natural Disasters

Many times, we have spoken about the natural disasters increasing in size and intensity throughout the world. Information regarding Earth changes has been woven into the content throughout this book. We think it important, however, that we speak in a succinct and focussed way about natural disasters since so many are struggling to understand the meaning of these events at a deeper level.

On almost every continent, hurricanes, droughts, floods, earthquakes and tornadoes are occurring with ever-greater ferocity. The powerful tsunami in December 2004, however, served as a wake-up call for the people of Earth. Graphic descriptions of the destruction and loss of life were communicated instantaneously through the media all over the world. They provided people with a personal view of the pain and suffering caused by the underwater earthquake and the tsunami that followed.

Millions of people reacted with an outpouring of grief, love, support and personal assistance that was unprecedented. As the initial shock passed, people began to ask why this great disaster had occurred. There was a hunger to know the underlying reason for such devastation and loss of life. Many questioned whether God was punishing them, and if so what could they do to ameliorate this pattern of increasing natural disasters. We have great love for the people of Earth. For this reason, we would like to give you our perspective on the escalating physical destruction occurring in your world so that you may gain peace and understanding.

There are three fundamental causes for these natural disasters. The first relates to the ongoing cycle of death and rebirth your planet undergoes as it moves through its many phases of life. It is part of the Creator's plan that your planet will provide a wide variety of experiences for advancing soul growth. These opportunities appear in events of joy and inspiration, the mundane activities of everyday life, and the tragedies and sorrows of pain and loss. They are all part of the human condition and provide a backdrop for the development of the soul – the warp and woof of humanity's experience on Earth.

Therefore, in one respect, it could be said that God plays a role in these disasters. This is so, but not out of punishment and retribution. The Divine Creator supplies a beautiful tapestry woven with the duality of life, reflecting what it is to be human. Humanity is learning how to love, laugh, cry and suffer – all part of the human condition. Only through the path of opposites will the human experience be indelibly etched on the fabric of the soul. As the incarnating soul rises above the horrors of disaster with courage and grace, life on Earth is irradiated with light and love, raising the vibratory frequency of the planet.

Secondly, the natural disasters at this time on Earth stem from the travail the great soul inhabiting your planet is experiencing as she moves through a most painful initiation. We have spoken of the manner in which this initiatory process is affecting Mother Earth. We ask that you consider what we say again from a personal emotional standpoint. She is in great pain, which is reflected in the turmoil that surfaces through many varied kinds of natural disasters.

By connecting emotionally with her, you will start to feel a more profound awareness of who you are in relation to the entity that has provided a home for you. It is essential that souls incarnating on Earth develop an expanded view of themselves from a planetary, galactic and universal perspective. Mother Earth is willing to go through the pain of expanded consciousness in order for you to grow in awareness.

Through loving prayers and directing positive energy into her core, you can assuage her suffering. She will continue to thrash in pain until her initiation is complete. Love her, respect her and support her. When the period of natural disaster ends, a beautiful rainbow will appear as a promise to the Earth and her inhabitants that a new day has dawned – one filled with promise and hope for all.

The third cause for the increasing catastrophic disasters rests with the people inhabiting your planet. The escalation of anger, greed, strife, and warfare that has spread throughout the Earth is contributing to the increase of severe weather conditions in many locales. In our first book, *Dreaming a New World,* and in this book as well, we have spoken about the effect that destructive negative emotions have upon the weather conditions in a given area.

People vibrating positive energy and living in harmony create benign atmospheric conditions, whereas conflict and strife generate a turbulent forcefield that can erupt into destructive natural disasters. If political wars continue to escalate, they will contribute to the imbalance of weather in various areas of the globe. We would like to emphasize, however, that the people residing in an area impacted by any of these misfortunes might not have been the cause for what has transpired.

The Earth's geological makeup is similar to that of the human body. Just as the body has a circulatory system carrying the blood through capillaries, veins and arteries to every extremity, so also does the Earth have a similar process of moving its energy through a grid of light encompassing the entire planet. If you were able to see the Earth as we do from the realm of spirit, you would observe radiating channels of light transporting energy to even the most isolated and remote areas.

This planetary grid can bring turbulent energy to a land not responsible for creating it. Just as cancerous cells migrate through the human body from the place originally producing them, so too can a geographic location experience severe weather conditions when the people of that area have not been the generating cause. This is a most important concept that we present for your consideration.

The people of Earth have a responsibility for bringing peace and harmony to the planet. Just as humanity is one with all life throughout your universe, so too is there a symbiotic relationship between the people of Earth and the planet that sustains them. When people create disharmony and discord in one area of the globe, the negative vibratory field can move throughout the planetary grid to surface in another locale not connected to the site of origin.

We ask that the people of Earth begin to understand how all of life is interconnected. Then you can take responsibility for the health and welfare of the planet and everything that lives and breathes on its surface. When this change in belief and behavior occurs, a new day will dawn – one carrying a new vibratory energy of peace and love. The natural disasters will lessen and assume their rightful course in the cyclical life of the Earth. Trust in the divine order and harmony of the Creator's Plan. You will always be loved and supported, no matter what is happening. Face with courage and dignity whatever life brings. At an unseen level, your life is unfolding with everything needed for your highest good.

# Earth's Role as a Living Library

Let us speak further about the state of health of your planet. Earth has been the home for many diverse lifeforms down through the eons. It has served as one of the third-dimensional laboratories in the evolutionary Plan of the Creator. In your universe, certain planets within selected star systems have been chosen as locations for physical manifestation. They have been created to offer a dense vibration for grounding and anchoring records of the soul's journey back to union with the Creator.

These third-dimensional planets serve as libraries displaying in physical form the record of soul experience and advancement. They present a record for beings of all types to observe the progress of the universal life stream. So it is that many other forms of life come to these living libraries to observe, study, learn and grow in their knowledge of the soul's journey. This is why the history of Earth's cultures contains myths and legends of humans interacting with different kinds of beings in a wide variety of ways. These were not fanciful tales told simply to amuse and entertain. They are accurate descriptions of real life events.

Does the fact that Earth is a living library cause you to think about your planet in a more expanded way? Does it give you a different view of who you are and what your purpose for incarnating on Earth is? Think of how you feel when you enter a library. Do you have a feeling of entering a sacred space where there is much important knowledge to help you grow? This is the purpose for which your planet was created.

Those incarnating on Earth serve as assistants to the librarian who is the soul essence of your planet. Gaia is the term currently applied to this great being who manifests the feminine principle in third-dimensional form. Gaia has been holding the spiritual blueprint for the soul's journey on her soil. As plant, animal and human life appeared on Earth, she changed physically in order to accommodate these life forms. Land masses rose and sunk beneath the ocean waves, offering new environments for human beings inhabiting physical locations all over the globe.

She knew deep within her soul essence that she was to provide a suitable physical environment for the unfolding of each step of the Divine Plan. And so she presented what was needed physically for the culture that would emerge. If a certain people required the rarified atmosphere of a high mountain setting to develop spiritual attributes, she raised the land to accommodate their life experience. If, on the other hand, a people's challenge was to grow through development of their emotional natures, she provided an ocean setting where living close to water would enhance this type of human growth. Or if a people were to ground a new principle for human development, she would offer the beautiful isolation of a desert to enhance the refining process for their cycle.

For many eons of time, advanced beings on your planet charted the passage of time and the placement of constellations in the heavens. Astronomical observatories of many different shapes and configurations still exist in a wide variety of locations throughout the Earth. Pyramids, ziggurats, stone circles, and raised platforms of all types were physical markers of great power on every continent. They were used to identify the changing positions of the stars and their movement in the heavens. When one sees the difficulty and complexity required in building these observatories, it is clear that the charting of heavenly bodies was an extremely important activity for the ancients. Why was this so? The reason contains knowledge vital for those currently living on the Earth.

The planets, constellations and star systems in your galaxy influence the Earth in a direct energetic way. All matter exists in a divine, connected dance of life, interacting as parts of the body do within the human form. You might say that your galaxy is a body of energy containing many different segments, all of which constitute a part of the whole. The ancients on your planet knew this, and so they needed to identify what the other parts of their galactic body were doing. They understood that each physical planet and star system exuded a molecular energy field interpenetrating the Earth with rays containing the spiritual essence of that planet or star system.

Over centuries of observation and probing the depths of space with their minds, the highly advanced beings on Earth were able to identify the spiritual energy fields of your solar system's planets, as well as the major constellations within your galaxy. They learned how their placement impacted the energy body of the Earth itself. But most importantly, they identified how the spiritual energy of other planets and star systems influence the behavior of human beings residing on Earth.

The ancients had a practical aspect to their study of the heavens. They wanted to know how their everyday lives would be impacted by the position of heavenly bodies within the galaxy. Since this information was critical to them, specific people within the culture were assigned the rigorous task of observation, record keeping and communication. Very often these individuals were priests, such as those in the land of the Maya who were in charge of the Long Count – a collation of heavenly star maps compiled over long periods of time.

The Earth's feminine soul essence has been nurturing and supporting all life forms existing within her forcefield since the time of the planet's creation. Indigenous peoples have always honored this great being whom they call their Mother, knowing that she is responsible for their ability to live and grow in this world. Down through the eons, they have held rituals and religious observances to show their love and appreciation for her service to them. The first wave of souls has existed in the Outback of Australia for millennia, performing the spiritual practices that pulsate with the heartbeat of the Earth.

Many other people located on your planet connect to Mother Earth, resonating to the throb of Oneness that emanates from her powerful essence. They have taken on the assignment of grounding the knowledge and awareness of the ancient wisdom in every area of the planet as we move further into the years ahead. In the last four thousand years, however, this knowledge of a spiritual entity inhabiting the Earth has sunk into the unconscious of most human beings. The people considered primitive by the technologically advanced cultures on Earth have maintained their practices of worship towards Mother Earth, keeping the drumbeat of awareness alive at a subliminal level for all others. However, recently the recognition that a great spiritual being is wearing the physical mantle of the planet has surfaced again. It is now time for a large segment of humanity to regain the awareness of the few.

In order for the human race to take a step forward in their spiritual journey, people must connect directly with the soul essence of Gaia, their mother. The old way of Divine Oneness will flourish again on this planet, as human beings move forward en masse into this all-crucial period of initiation. There is a beat that pulsates continuously, sending a vibratory message to all those who are encoded to hear it. We ask our readers to attune yourselves to the beat. Let it flow consciously through you. It will heal, strengthen and uplift you, enabling you to move up the next step on the spiral of life.

Incarnating souls need to see how their lives are made possible through the nurturance and support of this great being. They also must realize that they bear the responsibility for honoring and upholding her highest good, even though it may run counter to their own wishes or desires. At the present time, countries with advanced technologies have developed a wide array of machinery that is used to reconfigure land to suit their purposes. Seldom if ever is Gaia consulted to see if the proposed work is in harmony with her wishes. On the contrary, what often amounts to desecration is initiated and performed without the slightest consideration for its impact on Mother Earth.

Offshore drilling, mining, hydroelectric dams, nuclear detonations, and housing and highway projects have seriously affected Gaia to the degree that she is suffering agonies, both physical and spiritual. The impact of multiple wars and military actions being carried out on her surface also adds to her pain in substantive ways. Her basic health and wellbeing is deteriorating rapidly. As she thrashes in attempts to reestablish balance, there is a corresponding increase in physical disturbances and natural disasters of all kinds throughout the globe. These are outer manifestations of her inner travail.

We wish to emphasize here that the severity of these natural disasters is going to continue and increase until human beings recognize the harm they are doing to the Great Spirit inhabiting their planet. People must start to honor her and directly connect to her soul essence. How can a person establish this connection? Start in your own back yard with land that you own personally or currently occupy. Do not add or take out any thing that is growing without asking Gaia if it is for the highest good. If a sense of the acceptable treatment for the land comes to you, honor it, knowing that you have been in contact with some aspect of the Mother herself.

Start to think of yourself as a partner in a co-creative relationship with Gaia – a relationship that has as its basic premise love and respect for all beings and the land itself. Then expand this awareness to others so that they too can join in honoring this Great Spirit who provides our basic sustenance with such unconditional love. Pray to her and for her. Once again we emphasize that you send energy to her daily by visualizing a green cloud enveloping the Earth, healing and restoring her to her former state of wellbeing. In order for humanity to be part of a New Heaven and a New Earth, we must reconnect to the Mother who loves and supports us every day of our lives!

## A New Heaven and a New Earth

We have spoken often about a new Heaven and a new Earth. This state will emerge as many souls on the Earth plane raise their consciousness and connect with us on the realm of spirit. You may ask whether Heaven will also be changed as Earth ascends up the spiral of life. Our answer is yes. As your planet transforms itself to a higher vibrational frequency, a shift will occur thoughout time and space, impacting all realms in the many universes of the Creator. For, you see, all creation is interconnected like a beautiful mosaic, shimmering and shifting in a divine dance of beauty and transformation.

Each and every increase in human consciousness results in molecules of light being reflected throughout all the realms of spirit. That is why we constantly emphasize the importance of raising one's vibrational frequency through loving thoughts and actions, as well as the spiritual practices of prayer and meditation. When one expands consciousness, more light enters one's force-field, reflecting and refracting molecular beams of a higher vibrational tone that are received by all other forms of life in the universe.

These beams penetrate and help elevate the many realms or dimensions that are commonly referred to as Heaven. The word "elevate" is accurate here, because all of life in every universe is in the process of ascending to a higher vibratory level. Heaven, or the realm of spirit, as we call it, consists of all the dimensions above that of Earth. As Jesus the Christ said so beautifully, "In my Father's house there are many mansions." He used the analogy of a house to describe the different spheres within the heavens of the Creator.

All life in every universe and on every dimension is directly interconnected. That is why any change, whether for the better or worse in your world, impacts and affects the rest of life in the other dimensional realms. We ask that our readers reflect on this information. At the present time, a few souls on Earth are beginning to realize how deeply their thoughts and actions affect themselves, others about them and even their physical environment. Very few know that they have an impact for good or ill on the unseen realms of spirit also.

It is true that the higher one ascends through the planes of spirit, the purer and more refined the vibrational energy of each realm becomes. But those incarnating on the Earth plane are linked to the higher dimensions, no matter how light-infused that higher plane is. All life in the universe exists in a unified field that is interconnected at a basic molecular level regardless of what the outer expression is. Therefore we ask that you attune to the higher dimensions. Know that you are connected to them whether you realize it or not. Start to honor your God-given responsibility to assist in the creation of a new Heaven and a new Earth!

# Cycles – Spiritual Patterns of Death and Rebirth

We would like to address human behavior, which at the present time is out of balance and harmony. As powerful planetary and galactic forces are impacting the Earth, human beings are being affected in a direct and disturbing way. They seem to be functioning within a forcefield of turbulence and ongoing disruption. Dissolution and disintegration are the order of the day. For those that do not understand the positive aspects of the dying process, it is truly an unsettling time.

To comprehend the forces at work here, it is necessary to consider in depth the vibrational dynamics of cycles. At the beginning of any cycle, there is an outburst of creative energy of the highest order that brings the cycle into being. It contains all characteristics of the major elements that will manifest during the cycle. The archetypal pattern of the cycle exists in its most pure form at the time of its creation. This pattern contains the Idea of the whole and projects this form into the entire time frame of the cycle.

As the imprint of the Idea comes into being, the power of the initial intent grows in strength. It moves forward with great force, propelled from its source and moving toward the most complete representation of its original idea and intent. At a certain point in the cycle, the highest level is reached and experienced by all of those participating in the unfolding of the cycle. This is the zenith or peak for which the cycle was created.

Once the zenith has been achieved, the human experience is registered in the soul knowing of all those beings participating in the cycle. The purpose of the cycle has been achieved, and the final portion of the cycle begins to unfold. This part of the cycle has a very different energy expression than the creation and manifestation portion of the cycle. The high level of intensity starts to diminish, slowly but inexorably. The underlying vibrational pattern that has been the fuel and sustenance for the cycle begins to wane. The death of the cycle has begun and will move forward to its completion, however long that may take.

This final portion of the cycle has clearly identifiable characteristics. The highest expression of the cycle at its outset cannot be revisited. All that was possible at its beginning can never be reclaimed, because the time for highest delineation is over. To truly understand the concept we are presenting here, think of the wave that originates in the ocean and rises to a beautiful crest of power and grace. Once that peak is reached, the wave crashes and dissipates into the water to form the elements of a new wave that has not yet started to form.

When the wave has reached its crest, the height of its expression has been reached and can never be regained. Its only action from that time on is to end its flow and merge with the whole, giving its elements to the creation of a new and different wave. The final action of the wave is dissolution and merging with the whole, a process epitomizing the final stage of every cycle.

Another example can be found in the waxing and waning of the moon. The potential for each cycle of the moon is found in the dark of the moon, for here is its greatest power. Then the moon moves forward to its full phase, where all the light and potential contained during its seedtime is expressed. After that manifestation is finished, the light of the moon begins to wane and finally ends the cycle. Some people have recognized that the waning time of the moon is not propitious for the beginning of an endeavor. The energy flow is not that of creation or building. It is one of dissolution or ending.

In the coming years of this century, the role of energy flow will be much more widely understood. Along with this awareness will come the recognition of how all life on this planet exists within a cyclical matrix. With this knowledge will come the understanding of where one's world is in the cycle of unfolding. Then human beings can live consciously, trusting that life is following the Plan of the Creator and is in Divine Order.

## The Unfolding Cycle of the United States

To know at a deep level that all existence is part of a series of unfolding cycles expands one's consciousness in a direct and meaningful way. Generally, cycles relate directly to the concept of time. Time starts with a second, expands to a minute, then moves to an hour, day, month, year, decade, century and into infinity. These periods are all cycles within ever increasing cycles of larger and greater duration. Each segment of the cycle relates to its larger and smaller segments, constituting a spiral of ever-increasing size and dimension within the whole.

To understand also that one exists within this framework connects one to the essence of his or her environmental matrix in a conscious and tangible way. In order to incorporate this concept into soul awareness, let us look at the unfolding cycle of that entity known as the United States of America. Its democratic form of government sprang from a new and revolutionary idea – that of individual rights and freedoms, with equality, liberty and justice for all of its citizens. In the history of humans on the Earth, no nation had been founded with such high precepts as its guiding principle.

At the outset, the United States was dedicated to a new form of governance, constituting a great experiment in human development. The idea of equality, liberty and justice for all spread throughout the globe, raising the hearts of men and women everywhere. And so it was that a steady stream of immigrants came to the shores of the United States to join in the creation of a new society, which offered hope and opportunity for everyone. The Constitution of the United States provided a written framework from which the American ideal would flourish and prosper.

In the centuries after its formation, the United States expanded its physical boundaries to the Pacific Ocean, Canada and Mexico, forming a cooperative structure of independent states that recognized a greater authority as its governing body. The willing participation of these states within a greater whole was unheard of in a day when war and conquest were the primary ways countries or nations joined together as one. Down through the years, the United States grew in power, strength and influence.

The zenith point for this country was the fifty-year period in the first half of the twentieth century. The role the United States played in the two World Wars was its finest hour. In both wars, the United States joined with other nations to prevent worldwide conquest and domination by aggressive military powers. The United States played the role of leader in forming a cooperative union with other countries to prevent the subjugation of thousands of people throughout the Earth. Even though warfare runs counter to the Universal Law of Love and Respect, the United States' role in preventing world domination by the powers of tyranny was a necessary effort on behalf of peace and freedom.

It gave of its physical and human resources, performing an incomparable service to humankind on the planet. After the Second World War, the United States again dedicated itself to the rebuilding of Europe and Japan, a course of action unknown in the annals of war and conquest. The participation in the two World Wars and their aftermath exemplified in practical application the principles upon which the United States of America was founded.

It is important to consider carefully the cycle surrounding the life of the United States of America as a country. Just as all individuals and nations exist within a cyclical matrix, so too does the political entity known as the United States. For many Americans, it would appear that the United States is currently at the apex of its power and influence. Its strength economically, militarily and politically seems to hold it above every other nation in the world.

And yet if one could see from the standpoint of cyclical awareness, it would become immediately evident that the United States has entered the waning or dissolution phase of its political reality. You might wonder how this could be, since the United

States is the dominant superpower in the world. Think of the caterpillar, which appears to be solid and substantial as it nibbles away at a leaf in a tree. What cannot be seen is that the caterpillar is starting the dissolution phase of its existence. Internally its physical structure is beginning to break down and dissolve into the matrix for a higher form of animal life – the butterfly.

This analogy aptly describes the United States at this time. The high principles that formed the foundation for this great country are being eroded and replaced by their opposites. Where there was freedom, there is now restriction of rights in a wide variety of ways. Surveillance of many areas of life is becoming the norm. In the name of security and protection, the powers of the government are upheld over the rights of the individual in a vastly increasing takeover unprecedented in the history of the United States. The cornerstones of the internal fabric of the country are starting to dissolve in the onslaught of governmental control and dominance.

Returning to the analogy of the caterpillar, even though the caterpillar appears to be fine, it is dying from within — not unlike the salmon that is swimming upstream to spawn as its final act of giving new life to its yet unborn offspring. The very fabric of American society is disintegrating as it assumes a more military stance worldwide. The principles of freedom, justice and equality cannot flourish when military domination becomes the overriding aim of a government. Slowly and inexorably the disintegrative process continues, while Americans are being reassured of their power and strength in a way that does not reflect the reality of the situation from an energetic or cyclical standpoint.

The United States is currently the most powerful country on Earth, and so it would seem that it is at the height of its development and influence worldwide. However, from the perspective of spirit, the United States has entered the waning or dissolution phase of its political existence. How could this be, you ask? Outwardly, its wealth, political power and military might are superior to all. This is true, but when one begins to see with the eye of spirit, it becomes readily evident that the outward appearance is a façade covering a disintegrating core. The power and influence of this country was never meant to be long-lived. Its primary purpose was to birth a higher expression of political intent — one that brought forth ideals of freedom and equality never before part of the cornerstone of a political state.

These ideals are being seriously corrupted at the present time by powerful forces within American society that are attempting to dominate and control. These forces are eroding the principles upon which the United States was founded. Down through the long history of human development on the planet, this scenario has been played and replayed. Societies with a commitment for higher human advancement have risen and then fallen because of corruption and decay within. If this is the pattern of cyclical unfolding, you might ask whether this progression is inevitable. Our reply to you is no. Death and decay become a part of the dissolution process only when human beings disintegrate into greed and improper use of power.

Each country's political cycle presents the challenge of developing to its highest intent and then ending in a harmonious completion of a job well done. It is only when the society of any culture sinks into the negative expression of its spiritual blueprint that the ending of the cycle is painful. A perfect example of a positive completion of a people's cycle can be found in aboriginal cultures throughout the planet.

Many of these cultures are being infiltrated by the more dominant cultures around them; but they are conducting the change and possible end of their way of life with peaceful harmony and beauty. They are not fighting the forces that are replacing them. Instead they are disseminating the teachings and lesson of their human experience with quiet grace and dignity. They understand their task of transmitting the knowledge and wisdom they have attained so that it can serve as humus for the next culture moving into ascendancy.

Compare the ending of the aboriginal cultures with the present course of the United States. This country is attempting to achieve worldwide domination through power and military might, resulting in death and destruction in various areas throughout the globe. Of course, these actions are couched in terms of bringing peace and democracy to the disadvantaged; but the real intent is political domination and control.

The citizens of the United States are being tested in this crucible. If they can insist that their country return to the principles upon which it was founded, the United States will walk the higher road and provide a contribution of inestimable importance to the people of the future. If Americans fail to uphold the higher ideal, the end of political prominence for the United States will be painful indeed and will be just another example of a culture's inability to uphold the spiritual intent upon which it was founded.

The United States has accomplished much that will be regarded by people in the future as progressive and forward thinking. What it has handed down to those who will live in future times is idealistically of a high order. Its principles of equality, liberty and individual freedom have provided an evolved model for countries that will rise to ascendancy in the coming years.

We do not wish to imply here that the United States is approaching the end of its existence as a country. To the contrary, it will continue as a political entity for an extended time into the future. However, the United States is at a crucial turning point as it moves into the waning phase of its life cycle. Its people must guard against the corrupting process that has begun to unfold energetically. There are many ways that a country, or an individual, for that matter, can positively move through the latter stages of its cycle.

If one were to sit by the oceanside and watch the difference in the ebb and flow of the tides, the characteristics of waxing and waning would become evident. When the tide is coming in, there is a powerful current that brings the water further and further inland, covering the shore in great depth. The water symbolizes the abundance of creative forces that are available in the beginning phase of any cycle. These forces continue to build to the apex of the cycle; or in the case of the sea, until the appearance of the full moon, signaling that the highest peak in the cycle has been reached. From this point forward, the tides will start to recede, and the energy flow will diminish until the moon cycle is finished.

During the ebb of ocean tides, much of the land that has been covered by water is exposed. What the ocean has brought and deposited during the heavy flow is now revealed for all to see. Those caretakers of beachfront property know full well what task lies ahead of them during the time of ebb tide. It is a period of cleaning and clearing away the unwanted debris and preparing the beach for maximum human use. This analogy applies also to the dissolution time for an individual or a nation. The dynamics are the same.

As the United States moves through the century ahead and beyond, the best way for it to proceed is to clean and clear all the unwanted debris and corruption from its body politic. And why should it do this, you might ask. The answer is very clear. Its legacy will have much more power if the country can maintain the purity and force of the concepts on which it was founded. The Constitution of the United States was meant to provide a model for emerging nations all over the world in the coming centuries. If corruption, greed and misuse of power soil the purity of the democratic ideals upon which this country was founded, the positive influence of the United States will be diminished severely and will not reach the potential for which it was created.

# The Dance of Duality – From Conflict to Unity

For many, the experiences of these times are greatly unsettling. The turmoil and unrest throughout the world is an outer expression of the inner state of most humans on your planet. As we have mentioned before, all that manifests begins at the realm of spirit, then is reflected in universal consciousness and finally is transmitted into the individual minds of those residing on the planet to be acted out in everyday affairs.

No physical act ever occurs without conceptualization at the level of Universal Mind. So what are we saying here? We are simply bringing to your attention the importance of your mental processes as they relate to what happens in your lives. Nothing ever occurs without it first being reflected on the realm of spirit and then in your own mind. Many people think that events and individual actions happen randomly. They do not acknowledge that the Universal Law of Cause and Effect operates in every instance manifesting on the Earth plane.

Some, upon reading these words, will ask if humans have free will or are simply puppets dancing to the will of a Higher Power. This is a question of great importance, which we will try to answer as succinctly as possible. It is true that those incarnating on planet Earth have been gifted with free will. It is also true that there are powerful spiritual forces at work developing certain themes to be experienced by human beings as they move up the spiral of life. The development of your universe is not a random process. The Godhead has established the parameters that dictate the types of life encounters each soul will undertake — personally, nationally, and at a planetary level.

In the coming years, many people on Earth will learn to see themselves functioning within a larger spiritual context. They will know what that context is and how it is affecting them in every aspect of their lives. They will be able to connect with the unfolding spiritual themes and live them on a daily level as an expression of the Will of the Divine Creator, which they are manifesting in the realm of matter.

How does this occur in the world of practical human living? As an example, let us look at the past one hundred years of continuous warfare throughout your planet. Particularly, let us look at the escalation of warfare in the Middle East in the early years of the twenty-first century, which threatens to plunge the world into a Third World War. It seems, at the outer level of political interaction between nations, that countries and individuals are causing these events by acting out personal political agendas.

What really is occurring here, on a much higher spiritual plane, is that the Creative Force is orchestrating the theme of love verses hate, cooperation instead of competition, peace as opposed to war – all in the arena of learning how to settle differences.

The growing reality of peace is starting to permeate the Earth plane in ever-increasing intensity. In the earliest times of human habitation on your planet, people lived in harmony with each other and with the Earth itself. They were beings of high vibration and were always attuned to the spiritual plane in all that they did. Life was serene and peaceful manifesting the true essence of the Creator continually.

But as the ages passed, these highly evolved beings sunk ever deeper into the dense vibration of the Earth, finding it ever more difficult to recall their real origin and nature. It was at this time that rituals and religions developed to help these beings remember their connection to the Divine Creator and their true home. No longer was their attunement to the Godhead personal and direct. By then they thought that their spiritual experiences had to go through an intermediary who would solicit divine intervention on their behalf. Thus the control mechanism of religion and the priesthood came into existence and has dominated the religious life of humans on Earth up to this day.

It was from this situation that strife arose on a major scale. As the spiritual contact and recognition waned, individuals became more contentious, and personal conflict began to surface. Survival was paramount so the group dynamic suppressed and prevented any widespread aggressive acts between individuals. Such conflicts were just too destructive to the fabric of society. However, when towns and cities with their religious overlay of rituals and priests came into existence, the seeds of war were sown.

Warfare is the act of aggressive attack by one person or group upon another for the purpose of domination and control. In the earliest Golden Age on Earth, an individual or group would never consider hurting another in any form. However, as the incarnating souls sunk deeper into matter, they lost their spiritual awareness and began to initiate acts of aggression against those around them. Warfare became an acceptable practice for settling disputes and gaining control over others.

Why do we speak of this matter to you now? We do so because it is time for the inhabitants of Earth to look closely and thoroughly at the harm and destruction that warfare is causing the human race. The twentieth century, with its continuous pattern of worldwide warfare, was a most necessary period. The extensive pain and suffering experienced by millions of people throughout the globe brought the evils of war home on a very personal level.

In the first decades of the twenty-first century, the possibility of a Third World War is beginning to surface. People all over the Earth are being activated to prevent this from happening. The lessons of the twentieth century are starting to take hold. Many are awakening and remembering their spiritual origins. They no longer agree with the spilling of human blood as a way to settle disputes or differences with other people or countries. The evils of war, and the separation from the Divine Creator that occurs when people fight, are being recognized and rejected.

We ask all those reading our words to consider this issue very carefully. In order for the human race to enter the approaching age of higher vibrational functioning, warfare must be eradicated as a form of human interaction. Peaceful cooperation has to become the prevailing mode of discourse. Every awakened person first must develop peace and then uphold it as the only acceptable way for people to treat each other.

Love is the strongest force in the universe. Love cannot exist where there is hate, which breeds war. One of the fundamental lessons of the descent into dense vibrational matter is that incarnating souls must learn to retain the spiritual essence of love in every aspect of daily human experience. Spiritual growth and development cannot occur when one is operating in a hurtful way with others. This is why we ask you, our readers, first to rid yourselves of aggressive warlike tendencies and then maintain peace in your home, your community, your nation and the world. Then, and only then, will a New Heaven and a New Earth be available to the inhabitants of your planet.

There comes a period in every planet's spiritual growth and development when those living within its sphere of influence must take responsibility for their interactions with others. For an extended period, incarnating souls focus upon achieving their own desires with little consideration as to how their actions affect those about them. It is of little consequence in their way of thinking. They are totally oriented to achieving their own wishes. People who stand in their way at first are viewed as adversaries to be overcome. As their purpose becomes more fixed, they see them as enemies to be defeated at all costs. It is through this series of evolutionary phases that warfare has developed.

In the earliest times on Earth, incarnating souls knew that they were connected to the Divine Creator, manifesting in physical form. It was unthinkable that they might hurt a fellow soul in any way. Gradually this awareness waned, and the seeds of discord began to appear. It is important to remember that everything occurring in the many universes of time and space is in Divine Order and a part of the Plan of the Almighty.

You may ask how All That Is could ever allow war to be a part of the experience of Its offspring. The spiritual theme of your universe is bringing harmony out of duality. How can you ever incorporate the quality of peace into your soul knowing without immersing yourselves in its opposite? Therefore, it is necessary to experience the horrors of war to the deepest extent before an unwavering commitment to peace can be made.

The purpose of the ongoing wars of the twentieth century was simply that – to immerse the human race in the pain and suffering of war, while the recognition grew at the soul level that any harmful act against another was totally unacceptable. At the outset of the twenty-first century, warfare is not abating. In fact, the question seems to be whether the world can stop an ongoing pattern of destruction through war. But we ask you to remember that everything that happens has a positive spiritual purpose. Every war with its accompanying loss of life and property will help bring the inhabitants of Earth ever closer to that time of peace for all, which is unfolding in this new millennium.

## The Law of Manifestation

People are feeling the effects of the dance of duality, which permeates their psyches at deep, transformational levels. Fear and anxiety are becoming the prevailing emotions for those who inhabit the Earth plane. An ongoing dread penetrates the many sheaths of the human body, making it more vulnerable to physical, psychological and emotional illnesses. Fear lowers the vibratory rate of the electromagnetic impulses within the human body, opening it up to disorders of all varieties. This is why there is much sickness, especially within countries directly impacted by war and political strife.

The worsening condition of so many people will begin to create a desire for a different but higher expression of human interaction. A growing number of people are tiring of the negativity and will call for something more positive to manifest in their lives. There is a need for applying clear, rational thought to political strife and conflict. The spiritual level also must be reached in order to move conflict onto a higher plane of peace and unity. For any significant advancement in human affairs, ideas must originate and be reflected first on the level of spirit.

The Law of Manifestation operates in the following manner: any thing that is created on the third-dimensional realm of matter has a spiritual counterpart, which is reflected completely in a clear, abstract form. It is a blueprint that contains the essence of its reality before it appears in physical form. Consider the analogy of a house yet to be built. The overall concept for the house first appears at the level of pure idea in the spiritual realm of intent. The intent is to build a house — nothing more, nothing less.

The power of intent begins the creative process at the spiritual level. Once that has occurred, the mental process is activated, and eventually a plan emerges describing in detail what the house will be like. It is important to note here that nothing has yet appeared on the physical level of concrete reality. When the plans are finally approved, the building process can begin, and the actual structure of the house starts to take form. The emotional component generates the desire and motivating power for the hard work that must be performed to build the house. This is an accurate description of how the Law of Manifestation operates on the spiritual, mental, emotional and physical realms.

The clouds of war seem to be gathering all over your beautiful planet, fouling the air and polluting the vibratory forcefield of the Earth. What people everywhere are witnessing is the disintegration of the Old World. They may not recognize the significance of what they are seeing, but truly that is what is happening. The world matrix that has been the guiding pattern for over five hundred thousand years is dying, and the forces of war are among the destroying factors used to accomplish this end. We do not want to give the impression that warfare is desirable, for it never can be a positive solution. But it has been the primary way in which great change has been initiated on your planet for eons.

However, a new means of manifestation is growing with great strength on Earth. This new way does not require that war be the initiator of societal change. Instead, peaceful cooperation is starting to surface as the most acceptable manner for humanity to move up the spiral of life. The creation of the United Nations after World War II established the blueprint on Earth for the political structure that would reflect this emerging change in consciousness. And every year that the United Nations continues to exist, the imprint is strengthened.

There is a growing awareness in people throughout your world that war is an unacceptable method for settling disputes between nations. People are also realizing that they need to speak out against the horrors of war. They are starting to recognize their responsibility in bringing about the transformation of Earth from a dark and sorrowful planet to one irradiated with love, reflecting the light of the Divine Creator in every way.

Two factors are creating this awareness in the people of Earth. The first is the accumulation of pain, deeply held in human DNA memory banks and soul knowing, regarding the suffering that war brings. The second is the fact that humanity has moved up the spiral of life and now knows at a profound level that love and respect are the cornerstones of human interaction, not hate and willful force.

So we say to the many who are deeply disturbed over the unleashed forces of war, hold to your soul knowing that peace is the only acceptable way for individuals or nations to interact with each other. Pray for peace. Visualize peace and honor it in all of your personal dealings with others. Speak out continually about peace being the key to all interactions on the Earth plane.

Affirming the concept of peace in all that you do and are will help replace the old paradigm of war with a New World view of peaceful cooperation. All change begins at the level of Idea. As you think peace and incorporate it into your lives, you are manifesting a powerful imprint that will join with others to transform human behavior. You will be creating a new Heaven and new Earth that has been foretold down through the eons of time.

The great beings that have come to Earth have spoken about this shift in human consciousness. You, living on Earth now, have been given the sublime task of creating a New World. Embrace it and go about your work. Be an ambassador of peace in every area of your lives. You are greatly loved and supported always by the realm of spirit!

## National Initiation – A Crucible for Growth

The Earth is going through a major initiation which, when completed, will propel the people of your planet onto a higher turn of the spiral of life. Even though we have spoken about initiation earlier in this book, we would like to make sure that the term initiation is clearly understood by our readers. An initiation is a life experience that presents a series of difficult challenges to a person, group, country or planet. Through the tests of an initiation, the level of consciousness is uplifted onto a higher plane of awareness. Someone who is taking part in a personal initiation emerges from the experience expanded and wiser than he or she was before, transformed into a new being in many ways.

Let us give some examples of initiations, which humans experience in the process of their soul development. Deaths of loved ones, significant loss of any kind, major health crises, physical, emotional or mental attacks, and natural catastrophes are types of intense experiences that present tests to be overcome. In summary, we are referring to anything that causes great pain and suffering. As one addresses a major life challenge, the personal human capacities are stretched and expanded to cope with the issue at hand. When the initiatory process is completed, the person is irrevocably changed.

To give an example of a country's initiation, we would like to look at two countries that are currently going through initiations of major proportions. The first is Iraq. This country has been involved in an extended period of personal and national anguish throughout the past century. In 2003, it was invaded and occupied by foreign forces that have increased the suffering of the Iraqi people. We will not speak to the political or ideological issues that are part of this initiatory process. We ask, however, that you recognize what a major initiation Iraq is experiencing in human terms.

The people of Iraq have to deal on a daily basis with the death of loved ones; losses of their homes, their jobs and their abilities to sustain themselves; ongoing attacks creating physical health crises; and the constant awareness that their country's resources and natural beauty are being destroyed. The great agony of the Iraqi people is the sense that their world is spiraling beyond their ability to control or stop the process.

We ask that the reader of our words quietly attune to the group soul known as the people of Iraq. Can you not feel their grief, anger and frustration over what they are experiencing? For an extended period now, they have been subjected to domination by their political leaders and from outer forces invading their land. The discussion concerning this war generally centers about the prominent political issues of the day. And yet we suggest to you that the most important element in this unfortunate situation is the initiatory process that the people themselves are experiencing.

We would like to offer a glimpse into the future to see what the initiation of Iraq will mean to the spiritual growth of its people. They will finally emerge from their suffering wiser and more compassionate. The fierce pride that is a part of their national character will still be in evidence. But they will reflect back to the world a picture of how a people under extreme duress can display courage and the will to overcome the most horrendous of circumstances.

As the rest of the world continues to observe the nobility of the Iraqi people, more and more countries, organizations and individuals will respond with help and support. This process is already underway. A greater sense of world community will develop throughout the Earth, and many will join the initiatory process of Iraq and raise their own consciousness to a higher level of human understanding and compassion.

We do not want to give the impression that hurtful human actions by one country against another will end. What we do wish to emphasize is that the Earth and its people are moving inexorably forward into the awareness that we are all connected – that we are all one. We must deal with each other out of love and respect. It is no longer acceptable that we injure or hurt others. We are children of the One!

# The Play of Polarity

The United States of America also is experiencing a powerful initiation. The duality of the intense interaction between the United States and Iraq, which started in the year 2003, is mirroring the opposing sides of the same initiatory process. The Earth resides within a universe that is predicated upon the Law of Duality. Therefore, anything that manifests must operate within a matrix containing the interaction of opposites.

This universal law manifests in every expression of life in your universe by offering a play of polarity in each thought, word or act emanating from the people of your planet. For Iraq to find itself within a context of great sorrow and suffering, it is necessary that there be a protagonist to create the painful circumstances needed for an initiation. And so it is that the United States is providing the energetic matrix for the clash of duality required in this situation.

An important point regarding initiation is that the conditions occurring during the initiatory process are necessary to the soul growth of all involved. For the Iraqi people, it is time for them to move up the spiral of the Creator. Since they live upon one of the most powerful energy vortexes on the Earth, their role has great significance. They are keepers of one of the planetary gates to higher consciousness. This small parcel of land, once called the Fertile Crescent, has emanated a vibratory beat of tremendous intensity from the beginning of Earth's formation.

Back before the dawn of time as you know it, human beings were drawn to this area in order to ground and stabilize a portal to the higher realms. In recent years, the idea of stargates has become popular with the general public in movies featuring this phenomenon. Little do the viewers of these films realize the truth of what they are seeing. As the people of Earth start to interact with higher dimensions, they will be drawn to the energy vortexes that exist all over the planet. These areas are portals or gateways to higher dimensions. As souls relearn the techniques to reach higher realms, they will utilize the energy of these places in a more positive way.

The people residing in these vortexes have always had to contend with painful and difficult circumstances in their daily lives. The energy of their area is so chaotic and turbulent that they suffer and grow just living within it. The ancient peoples knew exactly where these areas were and made pilgrimages to them. But first they conducted extensive and careful preparations that enabled them to withstand the assault of the intense vibratory field they were to encounter. Now that knowledge has been lost, most people residing in these vortexes are completely unaware that they are being bombarded continuously with vibrations affecting them in all areas of their lives.

The topic of initiation is extremely significant at this point in human spiritual development. A major proportion of the souls now incarnating on the Earth plane will be experiencing initiations during the course of their lives. Therefore, we want to help them understand the significance of these difficult and painful experiences. Once they see the higher spiritual purpose behind these events, it will be easier for them to endure as they move up the spiral of life.

This same principle of initiation applies to the interaction between nations as they undergo circumstances that cause great suffering. Also, one must not lose sight of the fact that the Earth herself is very adversely affected by the negative actions of people for whom she is providing life and sustenance. So let us look again at the initiatory process involving Iraq and the United States. Yes, the United States is also in the throes of an initiation of major proportions. As we have said, your universe operates on the Law of Duality, which is the underlying principle for all manifestation of life within its energy matrix.

In order for the people of Iraq to experience great pain during their process of initiation, there has to be an aggressor so that the inexorable Law of Duality could be brought into motion. The United States of America and its participating allies chose to enter this play of consciousness as the adversary and catalyst for the unfolding of the initiation process. They are fulfilling the role of military aggressor against the nation of Iraq. We know that being designated aggressors will not be well received by the United States and its allies, since they claim that their attacks are justified. However, using a higher spiritual standard, any person, group or nation initiating direct forceful actions against others that cause suffering or death falls into the category of aggressor – no matter what the reason for the action.

Down through the ages, various people have initiated warfare against others for the loftiest of reasons. The Crusades of the Middle Ages provide a perfect example of aggression predicated on high religious principles. Whenever a person, group or nation attacks another, their aggressive actions carry a heavy karmic responsibility. Even though at the level of human understanding they think their actions are good and necessary, they must take responsibility and eventually atone for the pain and suffering they are causing. In accordance with the universal Law of Cause and Effect, they will some day be subjected to exactly what they are inflicting upon others – no more, no less.

The supposed rationale for the attack against the Iraqi people was to prevent the spread of terrorism and guarantee safety for the world – lofty goals indeed. But as long as these goals are accomplished through military action preemptive in nature, the Law of Cause and Effect is activated and will bring retribution to the aggressors. We know that our words will be very difficult for many to read and accept, particularly for those residing in the United States and Great Britain. But we must present our view in regard to what is transpiring on the Earth plane. Our purpose is to bring awareness so that the people of Earth can raise their consciousness and move up the spiral of life, ultimately to merge with the Creative Force of the universe.

## War in Iraq – Spiritualization of the Human Heart

We would now like to focus on the role of the United States as the catalyst and aggressor in this initiatory process, so significant to the rest of your world. The United States as a country was founded on the highest ideals known in historical record. Its dedication to liberty, democracy and freedom are of a more evolved human vibration than any country in past memory. Even though obvious expansionist policies existed during its formative years, the United States has offered a governmental blueprint that was more advanced than any other country on the planet.

As we have pointed out earlier, the United States is now in the waning or dissolution phase of its history as a nation. A process of corrosion or corruption of the principles upon which this country was founded has begun. Domination, manipulation and the misuse of power typify the political decision-making of the government. Greed and vested self-interest are the order of the day. And so it is that the shining principles upon which this country was founded are slipping away like the waning tide on the shore of a mighty ocean. We would like to say that this declining process is following a common cyclical course. However, there is an inherent spiritual challenge implicit in this phase of the United States' spiritual development.

The latter portion of any cycle can be manifested in a number of ways. This part of the cycle need not necessarily be negative. The United States could use its power and influence to establish the principles of democracy in a peaceful, cooperative and politically enhancing way. It could be a model and mentor to countries that are interested in establishing democratic political structures. This course would exhibit a higher spiritual expression than that which is currently being presented and would be of inestimable service to countries all over the Earth.

Instead the United States has entered an initiation process, which has caused great pain and suffering for Iraq. So where will this course of action lead the people of the United States? It will project them also into a state of pain and suffering similar to that of Iraq, but it will manifest differently. Initially, the United States will not experience the physical horrors of war conducted within its own borders. Instead, a growing number of citizens will descend into the emotional, psychological, and spiritual states of deep anxiety, divisiveness, shame, frustration, powerlessness, loss of guiding principles, and despair, as they stand by seemingly unable to stem the spreading violence in any meaningful way.

Within this crucible, the people of the United States have an opportunity for accelerated spiritual growth just as the people of Iraq have. They can absorb into the deepest levels of their personal consciousness the principles upon which their country was founded. It must be noted here that many Americans live within a country espousing highly evolved concepts, but they have not incorporated these ideals into their beliefs and actions toward others. And so it is that Americans who are known for their use and commitment to the automobile, have reached the point where "the rubber meets the road." In other words, proof of effectiveness does not exist until it is put into physical reality and tested. As an example, forcing a democratic form of government upon another country runs counter to the underlying principle of democracy, which insists on free choice unfettered by coercion of any kind.

It appears that the escalating warfare in Iraq may result in ongoing conflict for some time. The entire world seems to be teetering on the brink of hatred and death. Viewed from the perspective of the realm of spirit, which is a realm interpenetrating the plane of matter, there is an exceedingly high degree of emotional anxiety and unrest permeating the astral atmosphere all over the planet.

Earth, in its geographic makeup, has a direct correlation to the human body. Various locales throughout your planet correspond to the organs in the body and possess the same functions. The Middle East energetically is the heart of the planet. Many have wondered why three major religions have originated there within the past two thousand years. In order to spiritualize the human race and Earth, transformation and transmutation of the heart center of the planet is needed. The teachings of the founders of these religions have inspired people and raised their consciousness in a profound and direct way.

And so the agony of hatred and war in Iraq, which impacts the entire region, correlates to a human heart under dire stress. It could be compared to a person with incipient heart problems prior to a pending heart attack. The heart is the part of the human body that serves as a circulating pump, pulsing out the fluid that enriches and nourishes the entire body. It has always been associated with the love aspect of human existence. This is why three major religions, Judaism, Christianity and Islam, originated within such a small area of land once called the Fertile Crescent. Their teachings were meant to serve as spiritually uplifting and consciousness-raising messages of love for Mother Earth and all beings living on the planet.

But the ancient seeds of anger and hatred are still strong within the human condition. These characteristics must be changed to a higher octave of love and respect in order for your planet to move up the spiral of life. This is why this grave conflict is occurring in the heart area of the Earth. The love aspect of human expression must be transformed to open the way for a new human species waiting to appear. This species will function in a personally powerful way, always coming from a position of love and respect. These more advanced human beings can only come forth when a compatible vibrational matrix exists within the forcefield of the planet. Therefore, the battle in Iraq is, at a deeper level, a contest for the spiritualization of the human heart.

As warfare continues to escalate in that region, the sensibilities of people all over the Earth are being impacted and heightened. The suffering of those involved is evident daily through worldwide communication, which offers ongoing pictures and sound displaying the horrors of the entire situation. Now you may glimpse the importance of some of the scientific discoveries of the past two centuries.

Many spiritually oriented individuals express great distaste for modern technology. And, in truth, there is an ever-present danger that machinery may replace necessary human functions. However, if the products of technological advancements are used to serve the common good of human beings, then all is in divine order in the evolutionary process. Radio, television and the Internet are making it possible for people to see immediately what is transpiring in every corner of the Earth.

This capability of instant knowing is having a profound effect on the souls incarnating on the Earth plane at this time. No longer do people have to rely on the interpretation of events from other sources. They are able to experience from an individual perspective what is transpiring in any given situation. Developing this personal awareness is a consciousness-raising capability of monumental proportions.

In the past, people experienced the initiation process in a private, personal way. Now the entire world is able to move up the spiral of life because of the technology of worldwide communication. And so you see, our dear friends, this is just another example of the perfection of all that is occurring in universes of the Creator. To see and incorporate this awareness at the deepest level of knowing provides one with the peace that passes understanding – a phrase appearing in many holy works down through the ages.

Incarnating souls on the Earth plane must learn to develop a deeper trust about what is happening in their lives. One must learn to accept that every event, no matter how uplifting or painful, contributes ultimately to the soul's reunion with the Creator of All That Is. Knowing this provides one with a sense of appropriateness for all that unfolds in one's life. Is it not profoundly uplifting to know that there is perfection in the plan of the Creator? You see, all truly is in Divine Order!

# Duality – The Underlying Principle of Human Interaction

Your entire world is in the throes of a great dualistic struggle that is pitting people against each other in the name of religion, nationalism and politics. What is really at the base of these struggles is a commitment to a system of personal values. Many issues of primary importance are surfacing in people's lives in order to bring resolution to this longstanding dynamic of polarity, the underlying theme of your universe. Inhabitants of Earth need to realize that they live on a plane of duality and that everything coming before them will do so from a dual base. They need to know that this duality is not a negative thing. It just is what it is – an expression of the nature of the Creative Force.

The common approach for eons has been to fight the polar opposite and try to dominate and control it in every way possible. This way has never been successful for very long. It has just created an endless circular motion of swinging from pole to opposite pole, perpetuating a futile battle that never brings satisfaction to either side. Those incarnating on the Earth plane have not yet discovered the primary purpose of duality as an underlying principle of human interaction. They have not recognized the cosmic dynamic they are involved in. It is called, "Oppose what is different from you until you see that you both are One."

The final goal is to develop an unshakable acceptance for the concept of unity. It is impossible to incorporate unity into the fabric of one's soul knowing until one has struggled extensively in a polarizing system. How could a soul arrive at this belief without experiencing the futility of duality as a guiding principle for soul development? Knowing the importance of unity raises a soul up the spiral of life to a higher level of functioning. But without the challenge that duality provides, unity as a core knowing of the soul can never be reached. Duality is the spiritual framework that leads the soul to comprehend and incorporate unity into its soul essence.

Recognition of the truth we have just stated prepares a soul to function very differently in duality, which exists on every dimension within God's universe. To know that every important issue or human dynamic will move through two opposite poles on its path to unity is greatly expanding at a primary level of being. What we are saying here is that each side is entitled to love and respect for what it represents. Each pole offers important truths needing to be developed. These truths are stepping-stones to unity for unity cannot be reached without them. We would like to repeat this thought. Unity cannot be reached without reconciling opposing poles. The great challenge is to respect the opposite and incorporate as much of it as possible in a final unifying principle that reflects the whole. How does this work, and how can it possibly be achieved in this time of great struggle and travail on planet Earth?

Duality and polarity are the underlying themes of life in your universe. Moving though duality to unity is the cosmic game being played by all life forms throughout your current universe. Every time a new universe begins its period of manifestation, there is a core theme serving as the cornerstone for the life cycle of that universe. We repeat: the theme of your universe is called "Oppose what is different from you until you see that you are both One."

At the present time, planet Earth is engaged in a great struggle of opposing forces manifesting polarity on all levels – local, state, national and international. War and echoes of war penetrate the ethers surrounding your planet, reverberating out into the far reaches of your solar system and beyond. As we have stated many times before, all life is interconnected and impacted for good or ill by every thought and action, no matter how large or small. There is hardly a continent on the Earth plane where disputes or strife over differences in personal beliefs are not occurring, causing great pain and suffering to countless people.

But the greatest struggle of all has been between the United States, its allies and the Muslim world. The war on terrorism is rending asunder any attempts for peaceful coexistence and harmony between the East and the West. The polarity or duality is apparent to all involved in or affected by this great conflict. Each side sees the other as the enemy and is fighting a terrible war of attrition in an attempt to prevail over what is seen as opposite and evil in every way. This process causing human suffering and loss of innocent lives seems to be caught in an ever-escalating spiral of anger and hatred.

The struggle serves as a perfect focal point for our discussion regarding the cosmic game of duality. It is classic in all ways. The beliefs and ideals of each side are seen by the other as diametrically opposed in every way. The obvious conclusion drawn here is that what is different must be eradicated and removed in order to maintain safety and security for either side. The rhetoric and public statements of the United States government and Iraqi insurgents focus on the evils and faults of each other, without any attempt at listening to the needs or concerns being expressed by the other side.

Currently neither side recognizes that in some more profound way there is a deep spiritual connection between the two warring groups. If this idea were brought forth, it would elicit resounding denial, if not outright horror, that anything of this nature could be true. The opposing forces are enmeshed in the righteousness of their cause and have made no attempt to move away from that fixed position toward a more conciliatory stance. And so we arrive at the classic framework regarding the clash of duality. The obvious question can now be asked, "What must be done to bring the polarizing position of each side into the unity of Oneness?"

## Bringing Duality into Unity

When hatred and animosity exist between two entities, whether they are countries, groups or individuals, the power of the emotional energy is so dense that it is very difficult to introduce a new approach to the issues involved. Therefore, the first step in achieving unity is to dissipate the extremely negative emotional forcefield that has formed around the two polarized factions. How is this accomplished? The pent-up emotional energy begins to diminish when positive mental and spiritual energy is infused into the explosive situation.

As people begin to examine the issues involved in the conflict and question their validity, a new energy is directed into the confusing vortex of emotional energy, bringing a lighter, calming effect. The vibratory energy of emotion brings power and projecting force to any given situation. In order for emotion to be truly effective, clarity of thought and higher spiritual purpose must accompany it. And so it is that those individuals unleashing the power of emotional intensity bear a heavy responsibility for what they have created.

This circular motion can end only when the two opponents step up to a higher position where their conflict transforms into a unifying stance that they both can accept. In other words, they need to join and work towards oneness, although they would not see that term as an accurate reflection of the situation in the beginning. We have said that mental and spiritual energy must be infused into any polarized situation. How exactly is this done?

Clarity of thought occurs when abstract mental consideration is exercised in any emotionally dualistic situation. To ask questions and review the premises for actions taken brings a cooling element to the fiery situation at hand. Mental energy carries the element of air with its fresh and flowing qualities, which starts to break up the density of coagulated emotions. And so it is that any objective review of a polarized situation where the positions of the opponents can be considered carefully and respectfully will bring forward what is necessary for achieving unity.

Once the mental activities of objective, careful scrutiny have taken place, those participating must raise their consciousness onto the spiritual plane; for it is only in these realms that a new expression can be brought into being. You may wonder how the spiritual process may be achieved. The answer is through strong intent, visualization, prayer, and meditation. In the case of the war in Iraq, when citizens of that country and the United States begin to change their minds about supporting the war with its destructive aftermath, they will have to consider a different, more satisfactory solution. How can they raise their awareness to a higher level? Through the intent to find a better alternative, they begin to discern a more peaceful, loving way, and the idea of unity begins to come into being.

Whenever human consciousness rises to a more advanced spiritual level, it encounters an increased vibratory forcefield containing the love energy of the Creator. This highly refined molecular energy breaks down in a slow and nurturing way the harsh emotions found in hate and fear. The loving energy of connection increases the awareness of oneness. As this oneness and connection are felt more deeply within the souls of those in a polarized situation, the need for a loving solution grows and takes form. Intent is created out of this recognized need for a new and better course of action for all.

You may wonder how human consciousness raises itself to a higher level of expression. Prayer and meditation, accompanied by visualization of a better way for all, are the means by which this occurs. The deep pain of those enmeshed in a polarized situation and those throughout the world who feel at one with their brothers and sisters creates the recognition at a soul level that a spiritual solution must be found. Prayer and meditation are spiritual tools connecting humans to the higher vibrational energy of the God Force.

Many souls incarnating on the Earth plane pray and meditate. However, few are aware of how powerful these practices are, because they cannot see the rays of molecules moving from their auras out to encircle the planet and beyond. If they could see the beautiful shimmering cloud of vibratory love energy that emanates from them, they would know why they need to set aside time during the day and night to participate in these practices. Prayer, meditation and positive visualization would become common spiritual practices used to uplift and heal.

We would like to emphasize again that the spiritual plane affects directly the move from duality into unity. Polarity, the prevailing construct for the universe the Earth inhabits, uses a dual matrix to create its physical reality. This means that everything created comes out of opposing realities, which serve as the womb for manifestation. We cannot emphasize strongly enough how important it is for souls incarnating on the Earth plane to honor and respect this fundamental concept.

How often has someone said, "If only that person could think as I think, all would be just right?" Nothing could be further from the truth. This wish means that there would be a single base from which that idea would spring. According to the underlying principle of your universe, every act of creation must originate from a dual matrix in order for it to take form. Think of the birth of a child. Every human being on your planet is created from a union between the masculine and feminine principle. This basic tenet of life reflects the concept of duality at its most basic level.

It is important for those in incarnation to reflect on this fundamental truth. People generally see something different from them as negative and try to change it. They need to understand that dissimilarity is essential to the creative process and has to be included in order to achieve wholeness. Instead of fighting that which is different from us, unity could be achieved if we would just respect our differences and find some common ground upon which we can reach agreement. The shift from opposing what is different to respecting and incorporating it into a unifying oneness is the spiritual challenge for those souls inhabiting your universe.

For this reason, we have spent some time reflecting back to you this basic law of duality. When the human race reaches the stage where it no longer opposes what is different or opposite and instead strives for some unifying commonality, it will have made a giant step up the evolutionary spiral of life. Since it is time now for this progression to take place, a major worldwide polarization has arisen on your planet to serve as the vehicle for this fundamental learning.

Also, the polarities of love and hate and war and peace are ready to be addressed and transformed in the hearts and minds of human beings on Earth. A new age is dawning – one that is meant to be more highly evolved than your current period. Warfare has continued for eons on your planet. This hurtful human behavior must be transformed into a recognition that we are all one and therefore worthy of love and respect. Once this consciousness is widespread, warfare will cease and the Earth will move onto a higher vibratory plane where the acts you consider miracles will become the order of the day. Is it not truly a wondrous time in which to live?

The inhabitants of the Earth are preparing to move forward as a planetary group to a higher level of human interaction. The more primitive ego and power stances of today and the past must be transmuted into respect, caring and cooperation for all. In order to change long-standing patterns of behavior, tremendous power will be required to stop the forward motion and turn the affairs of humans in a totally new direction.

Think of the analogy of a train moving rapidly down railroad tracks with great speed toward an unknown catastrophe. What will it take to stop its forward momentum? Another train coming on the same tracks could create a crash that would stop and destroy both trains. A railroad tunnel could collapse and stop the train from moving forward as an act of divine intervention or human espionage. Or the engineer could stop the train of his own volition and allow the passengers to disembark safely. If any one of these scenarios were transposed onto the current world situation of escalating warfare, it can be seen how they could apply as probable futures for the human race.

The act of two trains colliding is analogous to the conflict between Western countries aligned against Muslim countries. It appears that the world is moving towards an all-out confrontation or crash of opposing ideologies and political agendas. The probable result would be profoundly destructive to both sides.

The aggressor nations could be directed through the power of world public opinion opposing warfare in any form to change their course. If this scenario were to play out, it would indicate that the human race had experienced an expansion of consciousness on a planetary level.

It is always possible that divine intervention from spirit could occur, but we advise you not to depend upon this assistance. The Creative Force wants Its offspring to learn through experience, until the lesson of peace versus war becomes deeply ingrained in the human psyche. The firm conviction that warfare can never be used in human interaction must be reached. It is true that a small group of people could perpetrate an act of terror so heinous that it would awaken people worldwide to insist on the ending of war. But the scars of this scenario could fester for a long time, ultimately plunging countries back into the repetitive cycle of war.

The final solution seems to be the most effective from a human and spiritual standpoint. There is an analogy to the engineer stopping the train through his own volition. If the aggressor nations come to the realization themselves that warfare against others is totally unacceptable and can never be used as a method of solving disputes, there would be the dawning of a new Heaven and a new Earth on your planet. Earth would join with the other inhabitants of your galaxy as an equal and co-creative partner.

Therefore, citizens of any country using warfare as a political or economic solution must stand firmly and seek peace as the only course of action they will support. Then, and only then, will the dark shadow of human pain be lifted from your beautiful planet, allowing it to emit the radiant light that has always been its true birthright.

The battle between the United States and Iraq exemplifies the dynamics inherent in the dance of duality and can be studied as an example for all conflicts between nations that will occur in the twenty-first century and beyond. In the summer of 2004, the polarization between the two countries reached a high intensity, with many people on both sides convinced that their cause was right and just. The duality was clear for all to see. There appeared to be no way out of this intensely bitter battle. And yet people in both countries were sowing the seeds of unity slowly and carefully, accompanied by many others throughout the Earth. How was this happening, you ask?

As people all over Earth observed the massive destruction and harm occurring in Iraq, the soul memories of millions were activated. They remembered at a deep level of consciousness the pain and suffering that war brought them in other existences, as well as in their current lives. The recognition was dawning on many that warfare is counter to the universal Law of Love, the primary tenet of the Godhead. People started to speak up, participate in demonstrations, and question the actions of the aggressive forces on both sides. In doing this, the first steps toward unity began.

The conviction continued to grow throughout the planet that what was happening in Iraq was unacceptable. More and more mental thought was applied to the situation with millions weighing and reviewing the issues creating the conflict. As this process continued, it started to impact the polarization between the two countries, sending the cooling air of reason into the emotionally charged conflict.

How long this process takes depends upon the will and intent of those involved. It is the duty of people on Earth to step up and apply objective, rational thought to the conflict between the countries. By doing so, the United States and Iraq will start the shift toward a new reality that will eventually evolve into a different course of action. We ask that those reading these words reflect carefully upon what is said here. We are suggesting that some form of participation by others throughout the Earth is necessary in order to bring peace and harmony to the devastated country of Iraq.

This dance of duality involves not only the countries participating in the war, but also other countries on the planet. They play an important role. No longer is passive observance without participation, whether it is mental or spiritual, acceptable. Humanity is about to take a step upward on the spiral of life; and the conflict in the Near East is one catalyst creating this great event.

Open your eyes and take responsibility for the crucial role each of you has in assisting the evolution of the human race. By the conscious participation of humanity in the unfolding of a new Earth, the Creator's plan will move to a higher, more spiritualized manifestation; and every one of you will have played a role!

# The Fourth Dimension –
# A Journey Into the Now

At this point in time, we shall begin to transmit a message of key importance for those living on the Earth plane. A great evolutionary cycle is drawing to a close. Life as you know it will transform into a higher level of functioning – one that cannot even be imagined by those now living on your planet. It has been determined at the highest levels of galactic intelligence that the Earth is ready to move forward into the role long intended for it since the beginning of creation.

This beautiful planet is a proving ground for soul growth and development. It was designated as one of those stopping places where time slowed to a pace commensurate with the activity found within its third-dimensional vibration. The gravitational pull of the Earth's forcefield creates a compact density ensuring that human experiences are encoded at a deep level of knowing. In order for true knowledge to be incorporated into the matrix of the soul, the life lessons need to be intense and unforgettable. This goal can best be accomplished at the level of the third dimension.

Throughout the universes of the Creator, there are many high-density laboratories, as you would call them. They are strategically placed so that the soul entity on its spiritual journey encounters them at just the right time. There is a pattern to the unfolding of all life. This pattern starts to manifest on the plane of mental causation. There the idea for any type of creation comes into being within the spiritual matrix of Universal Mind. The thought form starts to draw to itself like molecules of vibratory matter. These wave-like particles undulate and oscillate in a divine dance of creation beautiful to behold.

Slowly and inexorably, the idea, which began on the spiritual level, takes form and comes forth as a denser physical manifestation ready to activate life on the third-dimensional level. It then is drawn into the nearest third-dimensional forcefield to experience whatever is deemed important for growth and development at that point in time. Once those experiences have been incorporated into the soul's data bank, the soul moves upward for a new learning, which takes place in a different dimension and place within the universe.

Why do we speak of such abstract and seemingly esoteric matters at a time when human beings on the Earth are so absorbed in their personal, material lives? It is simply because of this emphasis on the material that we must focus on a wider, more expansive view of the soul's true condition. It is as though those living on Earth have been encased in a thick cloud, unable to see the reality of who they are and what really is happening to them. This is as it was intended so that the intensity of the Earth sojourn would make an indelible imprint on the soul's memory banks.

But now the cycle is drawing to a close. It is time for Earth inhabitants to lift their heads, open their eyes, and return to the awareness they possessed before they came into the Earth's gravitational field. You are children of the universe with knowledge and abilities far greater than you can even imagine. Listen to our words. Pull them into the deepest level of your soul knowing. You have been on a long journey — one that is not yet over. But you are making progress on the spiral of life. Get ready for the next great leap forward. It is truly a remarkable time, is it not?

## Guardians of the Flame

The present world is going through a process of fundamental change. A new wave of human being is slowly emerging and joining those who currently reside on the third-dimensional plane. This has been foretold throughout time by all the indigenous cultures strategically located in the energy vortexes of the planet. It is no accident that these holy ones live where they do. On every continent, there is an ancient tribe of people who appear to be primitive by the standards of the technically oriented western world.

However, they are anything but primitive in their knowledge concerning the realm of spirit and its interaction with the physical world of the third dimension. Their entire lives are interwoven into the Dreamtime, as the aboriginal people of Australia call that plane of creative idea where all that manifests is generated. From the beginning to the end of each day, they are always guided by the knowledge that everything in their world carries the life force of the Almighty and is sacred.

Their beliefs and practices create a vibratory rhythm that pulsates into the planetary grid, circulating a wave of balance and harmony, which heals and stabilizes the Earth. For thousands of years, this responsibility has been faithfully performed in every key area of the planet where these people live. They have always been clear about what Divine Oneness has requested of them and have faithfully performed their duty to the best of their ability.

Now the end of this age is at hand. The aboriginal peoples know this and have been preparing for the conclusion of their role as Guardians of the Flame. They are releasing information about their beliefs and practices so that they can be incorporated into the technologically sophisticated societies of today. If their ideas are accepted and assimilated, ongoing balance throughout the Earth will be assured. To help in the dispersion of their knowledge, educational materials, such as books and videos, have begun to appear offering aboriginal knowledge to the outer world.

Many of Earth's people are completely disconnected from the realms of spirit, which offer such beauty and richness to life at all levels. One of the characteristics of the coming age will be the continuous interaction that will occur between the higher dimensions and the Earth plane. The humans of the future will have expanded brain capacity, which will allow them to manifest all that they need and want. In order for this to happen, they will have to assimilate the awareness and practices of the aboriginal people into their knowledge base.

We ask that all readers of this book recognize and honor the role that the aboriginal people have played down through the ages. Seek any and all information coming from this source. Blend their beliefs into your lives so that you can start this expansion process, which will alter and restructure the very molecular alignment of your DNA. If you do this, you will begin to prepare for the coming of the new species, being birthed at the present time. Do you see the crucial responsibility that you have? Please accept it and join with the other pioneers who are helping to initiate this great step forward in human evolution.

## Emergence of a New Human Species

Many living on Earth at this time are prototypes of a new human species. Their ability to be aware of the spiritual realm and actually experience some aspects of its existence places them in the group of humans who are helping to birth a new type of being on Earth. The electrical wiring of their bodies has been modified somewhat, allowing a higher vibrational energy to enter their system. Also, the pathways of their brains have a different configuration from the average person.

This slightly unusual brain pattern will be the norm for those coming onto this plane in the future. Those individuals who have expanded their "sixth sense" have modified the physical structure of their brains but generally are unaware of it at the present time. However, as this process of human change continues, science and medicine will learn through researching the human brain that it has changed and expanded.

There will be a growing recognition that the human brain has increased its usage from ten percent to twenty or thirty per cent of total capacity. This knowledge will emanate from two sources. The first will occur as human brains are examined to identify the cause of illness. The second will come from the behavioral sciences, as rapidly expanding mental abilities emerging in the human race are identified.

People all over the Earth are meditating and raising their consciousness to a higher plane. This is causing the actual physical structure of their brains to be reconfigured. Unused pathways are being activated. Dormant areas of the brain are literally opening up to new impulses, which are then incorporated into overall brain function. The best way to understand this phenomenon is to look to the computer. When new software is introduced into the computer, its capability and output increases to the extent of the software's programming.

And thus it is so with the human brain. When individuals develop advanced ways of thinking and acting, they are introducing new patterns into human behavior. In effect, they are programming their brains with software, which is adding to their overall brain capacity and functioning. We ask you to reflect carefully on what is being said here. The people living on the Earth at the present time are offering themselves to the human evolutionary process as progenitors of a newly emerging species – one whose DNA will differ dramatically from the humans of today.

What is the significance of this information to the reader of these words? We, who have been the guiding force of growth and change for many eons in your world, are asking you to realize that you are now entering the evolutionary process in a direct and meaningful way. You are becoming co-creators with Divine Oneness as physical matter is becoming irradiated with the light of spirit. The human brain is the pivotal point of this transformation. It is the human reflector of this spiritually enlightening process.

Human beings now need to know clearly that the steps they are taking to raise their level of consciousness have greater ramifications than they ever thought possible. Join with the cosmic dance up the spiral of life. It will lift you above your present abilities into a realm far beyond what you ever thought possible.

# The Pathway to Higher Realms

The pathway to the higher realms or dimensions is really very easily accessed. All dimensions exist in a fluid and interconnected molecular state. They interpenetrate each other's space in a direct and commingled way. What differentiates one dimension from another is the speed with which the vibratory waves move within a given forcefield. The idea that spiritual realms exist far removed from each other is inaccurate. Reality is a diverse and interactive multidimensional field, which can be entered only by beings whose vibratory rate is within the given frequency of the particular dimension in that field.

As the technology of your scientific world develops, the accuracy of what we have just said will be discovered in measurable ways. This discovery is close at hand. It is now time for human beings to move out and away from Earth and explore the galaxy with its myriad of life forms. Human beings also are ready to move out of their current mode of third dimensionality and move upward into the fourth, fifth, and sixth dimensions of time, space and mental causation. However, there are certain basic steps that must be taken in preparation for such an inner journey.

The first step involves a personal acknowledgement and recognition that the universe is comprised of numerous levels of existence. Each one provides a correspondingly complex set of experiences, which helps the soul entity grow and develop on its way to reunion with the Creator of All That Is. As the individual soul participates in each dimension's offerings, the vibratory rate accelerates until it reaches a point in velocity where an upward motion raises it up the spiral of life. As the spiral turns, the soul entity leaves its current dimension and moves into the next higher one.

Just as the soul is about to leave its current level, there is a recapitulation and review of all that has occurred there. When that has finished, the knowledge gained is incorporated at a molecular level and is retained as a deep soul knowing – always accessible whenever needed. Therefore, in order for one to enter a higher dimension, the entity has to believe wholly that this upward motion is possible. Also, the soul needs to prepare itself in a variety of ways to effect this change in vibratory rate.

In the fourth dimension, time as it is experienced on Earth takes on a very different perspective. One of the first sensations that will be noticed is that time expands beyond what is known or experienced on the third dimension. Residents of your world think that time follows a line from past to present to future. That is not the case when one rises into the vibrational field of the fourth dimension. It is as if one goes through a vortex of energy at warp speed and suddenly emerges into a greatly expanded field of the Now where all events are occurring simultaneously.

One feels as if all that exists is within the vision of the viewer. This does not mean that one sees everything that has occurred, is occurring, or will occur throughout time and space. It simply means that whatever the viewer turns attention to will be seen in a much wider context of time. It will become readily evident that every event is interrelated to every other event in a tangible and connected way. Once one acquires this elevated view of time and returns to the third dimension, then words, deeds and actions will be seen in a totally new light.

This ability to see the Eternal Now places a strain upon the nervous or electrical system of humans from the third dimension. This effect on the physical body must be recognized as a natural response that can be overcome as one enters this new realm more often. Therefore, we suggest to those who are entering the fourth dimension that you form a strong intention to enter this realm and stay only as long as is safe and comfortable for you. Your soul essence will protect and watch over you, initiating the transfer back if you stay too long.

Later, we will cover specific steps one must take to move into the higher vibrational frequency of the fourth dimension. For now, we ask the reader to reflect upon the ideas we have introduced regarding this new view of time. One must release all preconceived concepts about time. For time never has been as you have been taught. It is an energy field that is all-inclusive. Nothing exists outside this field of the Now.

Once a human being experiences time in this totally different construct, the physical brain's pathways expand significantly. The ability of the human brain to quantify existence moves onto a much higher level of comprehension. The innate knowing regarding one's relationship to the universe and the Divine Creative Force shifts into a higher gear no longer suited to the restricted view of time held by those living on the third dimension.

This new experience of time will become increasingly familiar to the people of Earth as they start to move into the next higher dimension. The journey will provide the first in a series of startling changes regarding how life is perceived. Inhabitants of the Earth are living in a restricted and incomplete way. Matter is confining, not allowing those enmeshed in it to truly see what exists all about them.

Only when the dense field of the human body becomes more irradiated with the light of spirit will the third eye of expanded seeing and knowing be activated. Once this opening occurs, the depth of life existing on the physical plane will spring into view. Also, the pathways into higher dimensions will be evident and will summon the viewer to an exploration of them. These pathways are circulating vortexes of light and movement beckoning the viewer to them.

As one moves into these circles of radiating light, it is important to enter the opening without fear and with firm intent in order to experience whatever comes, without judgment or definition. Fourth-dimensional travelers will encounter forms, vistas, and situations, which will strain the credulity of the third-dimensional mind. In many instances, a guide will appear to accompany the inner space traveler on the journey. This guide will take whatever form is familiar or pleasing.

For a devout Christian, Jesus, Mary, or one of the saints or apostles could appear to guide the individual. For a Native American or someone of indigenous stock, it could be a god-like figure or a totem animal. For another, it could be a departed friend or someone admired but not known. But whoever appears to accompany the newcomer to this higher realm, it will be an entity who is not threatening and who will prove to be helpful. It is advisable for the person embarking on this journey to accept the services of the guide with appreciation. If this is done, a bond is established, and the journey begins.

The guide will stay as long as the companion wishes and will leave upon request. However, a guide is invaluable and is best utilized throughout the trip, particularly for the first few times, since the guide can explain in an understandable manner what is transpiring. It is difficult to prepare the traveler for the wide variety of unusual happenings that will present themselves. Only when one enters the fourth-dimensional realm can one know of what we speak.

As we continue with the description of the fourth dimension, you will begin to understand more fully the experience that many of you on the Earth plane will be having in the years to come. The increase of your spiritual practices and the breakdown of your molecular systems by the technology surrounding you are preparing you to move out of the third-dimensional realm onto higher planes.

Most of you have no awareness of the impact that modern technology has on your physical and etheric bodies. The etheric body, as you may know, is the vibrational energy sheath directly surrounding your physical body. It serves as a protective conduit for the universal forces that are continuously being taken into your system. In this etheric body, the chakras or wheel-like vortexes are continuously receiving and transforming the life force of the universe before it enters your body. The chakras provide a transmuting function, which steps down energy voltage to the level that the human body can receive it.

Since the harnessing of electrical energy and the numerous inventions that have appeared in its wake, a powerful but disruptive energy field exists in all of the countries of the Earth that are considered materially advanced. Any machine that is run by electrical power emits at a subatomic level a definite forcefield, which interacts in a direct way with human life in its immediate area. The physical body is constantly receiving electrical charges of a low but significant degree. These charges are slowly changing the body at a basic molecular level.

We would not want you to think that this process is entirely negative. On the contrary, the bombardment of electrical vibratory waves is breaking up the current bodily structure, which has become rigidly condensed in a form that cannot rise in its present state onto a higher level of functioning. So modern technology provides a most important service indeed. It is helping to transmute the existing human body into one that will more adequately meet the challenges of the newly emerging world.

We do not wish to imply, however, that this is a benign and positive process at all levels. The final outcome is beneficial since the universal forces, condensed into electrical energy on the third-dimensional plane, are helping to phase out an older model of human being so that a new and more advanced species can come to take its place. However, the destruction of any living essence is a difficult and painful process. This is particularly so in the dense gravitational field of the third dimension.

As the physical, etheric, emotional, and mental bodies of each human being begin to disintegrate in varying degrees, the psychic residue emitted into the atmosphere creates a powerfully negative forcefield affecting behavior, physical health, and emotional and psychological wellbeing. This disintegrative action with its attending debris causes turmoil and disruption throughout the Earth. It often appears that human behavior is going berserk, with peace and tranquility becoming difficult to attain.

But on a higher level of understanding, one knows that these things are the natural outcome of the process that is underway. We ask you to recognize what is unfolding all about you and take the necessary steps to protect yourselves from the harmful aspects of this transition time. What are the necessary steps, you might ask. They are the following: emotional release, psychological review of thoughts and behavior, strengthening of the physical body, spiritual practices of prayer and meditation, attunement to the realm of spirit, and spending time in nature restoring and rejuvenating your souls.

# Preparations for Fourth-Dimensional Travel

The first step that has to occur in order for one to move into the higher dimensions is the gathering of strong intent. This journey cannot be undertaken just because it might be an interesting thing to do. The individual has to know that ascending to a higher vibrational plane is an essential part of the spiritual journey. It must be embarked upon with a firm resolve to overcome any and all obstacles that might appear along the way. One must recognize that each experience will be necessary in order to move into closer contact with the Divine Creator. For this reason only should one attempt this course of action. There can be no other.

All souls attempting to go beyond the vibration of the third dimension experience a fundamental shift in their consciousness and personal energy field. The expansion in awareness is dramatic. They never will feel as they did before after they return to their present world. The heavier gravitational pull of the denser third dimension will affect them in many noticeable ways for the remainder of their years on Earth.

Then why would someone even consider participating in such an experience? The answer is quite simple. There exists within the makeup of each human being a soul that is comprised of the light energy of the God Force. The soul exists in a state of continuous attraction to its Creator's spiritual vibration. For this reason, the soul always is searching for reunion with its Source. It can never be content with its present state when there is a higher dimension beckoning it to ascend into closer contact with the Creator.

So, brave and adventurous pioneers of the spirit set forth on this journey into the higher planes. They know at an intuitive level that they really have no choice. They cannot do anything other than embark on the task that awaits them. It would be a negation of their personal integrity to refuse to follow their inner prompting. The wise ones start with a rigorous and thorough preparation. They know that they have to be strong physically, emotionally, psychologically and spiritually in order to survive with their human persona intact.

The journey into the higher dimensions is an exhilarating experience, but one that can be fraught with peril if the individual entering these higher realms is not fully prepared. Some time is needed for the person to become centered and strong on the inner and outer levels of life. Discipline must be gained through whatever means desired. The one who wishes to ascend must become balanced in four areas of life – physical, emotional, psychological and spiritual.

It is true that many, in this current day, are studying the practices of ancient shamans and are gaining a rudimentary awareness of the methods for ascension. But they generally do not participate in the extensive developmental process required to enter the higher realms without personal harm. To compound the matter, these unprepared ones offer to teach others when they themselves are not adequately grounded in the essentials of higher dimensional travel.

Therefore, we want to caution those who are interested in entering the higher levels. Slowly and carefully develop yourselves in the four basic areas listed above. Physically, the body must be able to handle the higher voltage electrical energy fields that it will encounter. Anyone who is sick or weakened in any way cannot withstand the forces, which will be generated by travel onto a higher vibratory plane. Therefore it is wise to tone the body's tensile strength, if possible.

To achieve tensile strength, the body must be physically fit both in weight and muscle tone. The bloodstream must be continually oxygenated with exercise of a moderate amount. Limberness is desirable, since electrical currents will enter the body throughout the journey, impacting the central nervous system and endocrine glands directly. A body that is supple can ride the vibratory waves in a safe and undulating fashion. This is why yoga and other similar body disciplines are advisable practices for everyone, whether they wish to enter the higher realms or not.

In the emotional area, a person has to strive for balance and harmony within the astral body. When one is in the throes of emotional upset or inner discord, it destabilizes the human psyche, which serves as the threshold for interdimensional travel. One needs to face the inner darkness of fear, grief, anger and guilt and release them so that the emotional body can become purified and calm. Centering the emotional body is one of the most important preparatory goals for this extraordinary event.

A clear, honed mental body is essential for maximum functioning. The thinking process is a constant comfort as one moves into the higher realms. Every situation encountered is registered at the mental level and constantly monitored by the human brain. This instant feedback system serves as the interpretive mechanism for absorbing the unusual experiences that are encountered. The development of the left hemisphere of the brain during the past three hundred years has been a great contribution to the interdimensional ascension that will become widespread in this coming century. The left brain function of practical, analytical thinking will provide an important element of mental stability for traveling to the higher realms.

Spiritual development particularly is required to guide and support the individual in an experience that is an assault at all levels. A solidly grounded belief system will provide the support needed while a vastly expanded view of the universe unfolds.

Trust in a Divine Creator. Those beings that act as emissaries will stabilize and uphold the individual throughout this life-changing event. Prayer, meditation and reading of uplifting books are essential preparatory activities for raising the vibratory level.

As one works in the four areas necessary for adequate preparation, a period of assimilation and incorporation is needed so that one can become truly centered and balanced. The closer one gets to reaching the goal of higher dimensional travel, the more testing experiences will appear in one's life. They serve as a honing force, refining and stabilizing the being at all levels for the new events that will unfold soon. So welcome the situations and people that seem difficult and trying. They are doing just that – trying to elevate you to a higher level of functioning so that you can move forward into the realms that are your true birthright and your true home.

In the future, many more humans from the Earth plane will be embarking on interdimensional travel. The term interdimensional is very apt, since the dimensions merge with each other in a vibratory matrix, which contains all dimensions in close proximity to each other. The factor that separates the various dimensions is the vibratory rate of each plane — the higher the dimension, the faster the speed of the vibratory waves existing at that level.

Therefore, in order to ascend into a higher dimension, it is necessary to increase the speed of the vibrational structure of the human body. How does one do this, you will ask. We shall attempt to explain this transformation in practical, concrete terms. Raising one's vibration starts with a strong, conscious intent. The individual must make a mental commitment to increase the body's vibrational speed. The next step requires quieting oneself by closing the eyes and releasing all thoughts from the mind.

The third step is crucial to the ascension process. We ask that you breathe deeply and rhythmically for at least ten minutes of time. This type of breathing brings an increase of oxygen into the bloodstream. It is then carried to the brain where an expansion of the capillary vessels occurs. This enlargement of the blood cells creates room for the higher vibrational waves to enter and begin the ascension process, like a balloon rising as more and more air is blown into it.

The increased oxygen in the brain creates the pressure that is needed to ascend from the third dimension into the next higher plane. From this point on, the experiences encountered are all in the realm of consciousness and are reflected and processed continuously in the human brain. The pressure created by the period of deep, rhythmic breathing will cause the human consciousness to pop from its bodily casing and enter a tunnel where accelerated speed of movement can be frightening. It is as this point that emotional steadiness and calm trust are imperative in order to continue.

## Fourth-Dimensional Reality

As one emerges from the tunnel of entry into the fourth dimension, the first impression one receives is the vivid color and form existing on this plane. It is as if the intensity of all one sees is increased one hundred fold. It is important to pause and accustom one's senses to this new and startling environment for a while before proceeding. A pure appreciation of the beauty encountered will stabilize the mind and emotions and help in the adjustment to this new reality.

It is at this juncture that a guide will appear to accompany the traveler on this remarkable journey. One is asked to acknowledge and welcome this entity and agree to the role this being will play during the experience. Then you will both proceed to an area of the fourth dimension that is pertinent to your spiritual growth. You will enter an environment that will be somewhat familiar and will reflect an area of current interest that you have on the Earth plane. The key significance will be in the role that time plays in this higher dimension.

You will move into an event that is reminiscent of one you have lived in this lifetime. The difference will be that you will enter a vastly expanded view of time as it relates to this experience. You will see that all actions connected with this episode are interrelated with what would be called your past and future lives on the Earth plane. But you will realize in a mind-expanding moment that all of these instances are occurring simultaneously in a beautiful tapestry reflecting your soul growth.

We cannot emphasize enough the significance that this first encounter has on the traveler to the fourth dimension. It will open consciousness and expand awareness beyond what you can ever imagine. To be able to understand the significance of an important lifetime issue in such a heightened way changes forever the view one holds regarding all of life. Just think of the impact this experience will hold for you. You will see with clarity and expanded vision the underlying purpose of a key area of your life. When you return to the third-dimensional plane, you will view this issue in a spiritually enlightened manner and deal with it accordingly.

The fourth dimension is a realm of great mystery and wonder to those who are unaccustomed to the expansion of time that comes immediately with entry into this realm. As travelers pass into the fourth dimension and meet the accompanying guide, the outer limits seem to recede endlessly into space. There appear to be no visible boundaries. All of time slows down and slips into a cadence that is rhythmic and comforting. Significant events appear and continue through to completion. The viewers clearly perceive that large amounts of time are passing before their very eyes.

They realize that what they are observing is not possible in the world they have left. Their awareness regarding the linear aspect of time no longer seems relevant or accurate. What they are seeing is miraculous indeed. Time appears to flow in a smooth and continuous fashion. They are able to see a series of events simultaneously and in its entirety. They also have a complete awareness of the significance and meaning of all that is unfolding before them.

No longer is there a question about the relevance of one's life. Every action, event, person or episode is recognized to be perfect in all ways. Being able to transcend the third-dimensional view of life raises awareness into a new and more expanded category of soul knowing. The individual experiencing this new realm suddenly gains a comprehension about the necessity for each and every situation, which has been a part of the Earth journey.

Guilt, pain, regret or anger concerning the current life begin to disappear. A sense of peaceful acceptance and understanding comes over the viewer, with a deep appreciation for the opportunity to live in the vast world of the Creator. There is a realization that the gift of existence is most precious and never to be squandered. Those individuals who come back from sojourns on the fourth-dimensional plane are forever changed in how they see themselves and the lives they are living.

Their appreciation and grasp of the human condition expand greatly. They now welcome every type of situation or person encountered on a daily basis, knowing that all in the world of the God Force is just exactly as it should be for their spiritual growth and development. A deep sense of acceptance will permeate into every aspect of their lives. So we encourage the reader to consider our words carefully. The pioneers of the new species will be the ones who brave this new reality with courage and daring!

## Multidimensional Consciousness

There are some cautionary areas regarding the interdimensional experience. Travel to other realms should not be viewed as a means of satisfying one's curiosity or gaining powers that would enhance the human ego before one's peers. Ascending to a higher vibrational plane is an experience that taxes every aspect of the human mechanism. It changes the molecular structure of the electrical system and rearranges the DNA in the human body.

The brain is particularly affected, since new pathways are created to register what is occurring on the more subtle vibrational frequencies. Ordinarily the human brain reflects only the experiences of the third-dimensional plane. In order to be able to serve as a conduit for the experiences of the higher dimensions, an expansion of brain capacity has to occur. How does this come about, you must be thinking.

It is at this point that we ask for your careful attention to what we are about to say. The increase in the function of the human brain will be the most important evolutionary step taken in the next two hundred years. At the outset of intelligent human habitation on the Earth, the prototypes for fully spiritualized beings incarnated at key locales all over the planet. As in all expression on the plane of matter, the perfect form is always created first to serve as a model.

In every life cycle on the Earth, there is a progression from the ideal form into a deterioration and disintegration, which then reverses itself and finally regains its former perfection. In many cases, the prototype appears only on the etheric plane of energy to hold the pattern while the evolutionary process unfolds. Since the remains of the first life forms are buried deep within the Earth or have been destroyed by cataclysms at the end of each age, there is no actual evidence to prove what we say. We therefore ask that you access your inner soul knowing as to the accuracy of our information.

The first truly human beings to walk on the planet had full brain capacity, which gave them capabilities far beyond what the people of this current age possess. They were able to compute, receive and transmit information throughout the universe at lightning speed. They could manifest with their minds anything they wanted in physical form. They possessed a highly developed sense of sight, being able to see events that were occurring anywhere within their world or dimensions beyond. They also could transport themselves to other locales, by disassembling their molecular structures and then reappearing in full form wherever they wished.

In order to achieve these functions that appear miraculous to us, these first humans used the maximum capability of their brains. When the cycle of deterioration began, the ability to function at the higher levels decreased. How this happened is part of the unfolding story of human life on Earth. In the past twenty years, new information has come forth that has broadened the knowledge base regarding the history of humankind.

There have been three different paths of creation that have existed on your planet. In the first, a perfect prototype appeared, providing the model for humanity to emulate down through the ages. The second path was the evolutionary one where life moved from the simplest form to the most complex, gaining a different type of experience from this progression. The third was the one that is slowly coming back into human awareness – that of creation by beings from outer space.

Soon the inhabitants of Earth will know, beyond a shadow of a doubt, that they are one life form among many who live in the worlds of the Creator. All of the universes of time and space are teeming with a myriad of beings experiencing what it means to live in the womb of Divine Oneness. In the near future on Earth, planetary consciousness will expand into galactic awareness. The time has come for the residents of the planet to move out beyond the confines of their solar system and become citizens of the Milky Way Galaxy, traveling and interacting with others in this area of the universe.

The information we are releasing to you is comparatively new and has not been made available to many Earth sources at the present time. The shamans of indigenous peoples have been the primary ones in the past that have experienced the fourth-dimensional realm in some depth. Their out-of-body journeys have taken them into the higher realms, as they sought information about healing, protection from evil, or prophecy regarding an individual's course in life. It was recognized in these societies, however, that those who served as shamans had a special propensity for this path and needed extensive training in order to perform this role.

Today, there are a few individuals in remote areas of the world who have been trained as shamans in the old, established manner. They are coming forth and making themselves available to select people who are meant to bring this knowledge to the outer world that humanity has progressed on its journey back to the Source. In the future, large numbers of men and women will undertake interdimensional travel, which was performed only by shamans in earlier times.

The primary reason that so many are now ready to ascend into the higher realms is the coupling of the universal ability to read with the vast array of books, which educate human beings on the planet and uplift their spiritual capabilities. At no previous period in history have so many been able to embark on the journey to other dimensions. So it is that the new millennium will be one of greatly extended human capacities that will develop the physical structure and function of the human brain far beyond what it is today.

We speak these words so that all Earth beings can start to think of themselves in an enlarged context. People must recognize the vast personal powers that lie fallow and untapped within them, awaiting the transformation that is now at hand. The great spiritual master, Jesus, said it so clearly when he told his disciples that they could do far more than he had done if they only believed it to be so. We ask the residents of this planet to lift your heads, raise your eyes to the heavens and move into your true heritage — the higher dimensions of time and space.

## Developing Extrasensory Awareness

We would like to speak with you now from a spiritual perspective about the current state of affairs on your Earth. The world you live in seems overburdened with conflict, strife, and outright warfare in many corners of the globe. People are being wounded or are dying in war-related events, creating much human suffering. Even those who live far from the war zones are being impacted energetically with feelings of anxiety and a general sense of uneasiness. Throughout the world there is a cloud of negative expectancy that hangs over the affairs of those living on the Earth plane.

From the realm of spirit, the energetic atmosphere of your planet appears diffused and partially hidden by darkening clouds of psychic energy. We must emphasize again that the thoughts and emotions of those currently in incarnation on Earth affect the very atmosphere with unseen vibrations. These vibrations spread like waves, encircling your planet with an energy field, which impacts all people of the Earth for good or ill. It is the rare person who can sense these energies and absorb or transmute them so that they do not adversely affect his or her thoughts or emotions.

We cannot stress strongly enough how important it is that the inhabitants of Earth increase their ability to recognize the energies surrounding them. The human body must become like a tuning fork, which reflects and refracts the vibratory essence of its immediate environment. This is the first step in developing extrasensory awareness. As this capability expands, a person will connect with what is happening in other locales on the Earth. Human awareness is meant to expand and include the ability to know and sense at a personal level the energetic patterns of existence throughout the solar system and eventually the galaxy.

You might ask why this ability is important. Humans are meant to develop a multidimensional capacity that will connect them with more highly advanced beings in the many universes of the Creator. Some of these beings inhabit forms different from the human body, but their abilities far exceed human functioning at this time. It is the intent of the Divine Plan that the inhabitants of Earth take a major evolutionary step forward by entering the galactic community, which is waiting to welcome them. In order to join this community, human beings must be able to know and interact with higher forms of life.

For millennia the souls incarnating on your planet have been functioning within a third-dimensional framework. However, during every age, there have been those who have been able to move into higher dimensions at will to access information and guidance for their fellow humans. These super-conscious souls developed the ability to travel into higher realms through lifetimes of training and practice. Many of their names are familiar since their service has long been recognized in the annals of history. For example, Jesus, the Buddha, Socrates, Pythagoras, and Confucius were a few of these highly advanced humans. They are examples of those in every age who were the lightbringers of their time.

In the many universes of the Creator, there are numerous levels of soul advancement and development. The Divine Plan will be completed when each soul ultimately returns to the Source that creates and sustains all life. Thus it is that we are connected at some level to everything existing throughout time and space. Each spark of Creative Force plays a role in the unfolding tapestry of life as It weaves a beautiful mosaic of love into all that exists.

For many thousands of years on Earth, the blueprint has been one of evolved beings inspiring the people of your planet who were like children learning from wise teachers. But now the children of Earth have reached the age of maturity and will be stepping forth into the role of teachers themselves. It is time for all humans to know that they can access universal wisdom, without relying on spiritual teachers to bring this information to them.

We cannot emphasize strongly enough the importance of what we say here. Souls on Earth are now ready to attune to and access the teachings they need without waiting for others to provide it for them. Think of how freeing this is! Humanity will change dramatically when it is realized that each person can access Divine Wisdom by raising consciousness and connecting directly with the realm of spirit. All that is needed now is to know that a soul has reached the point in personal development where it can connect with the higher dimensions through certain simple practices.

## Time –The Ever-Present Now

Time is relative and does not manifest in a past, present and future framework. Time is a holistic matrix operating out of the eternal Now. This idea is most difficult for beings in the third dimension to grasp. For them, the concept of time is compartmentalized into three spheres – past, present and future. This reality is so deeply ingrained within the consciousness of Earth's inhabitants that it resembles the hardwiring of a computer with essential data. Their view of time is fixed into a triune reality that identifies all actions as having happened before, occurring now or unfolding in the future.

From the standpoint of the higher dimensions, this is an inaccurate and flawed view of time. The first step for the soul who moves out of third-dimensional consciousness is to encounter time at the next dimensional level, the fourth. Here, all thoughts and actions are occurring simultaneously at many different levels of existence. How can this possibly be, you ask. We will try to explain this phenomenon so that your view of time can shift and grow into a new mental construct – one that is essential for travel to higher dimensions.

Why do we speak about the inhabitants of Earth moving into multidimensional consciousness? For many eons, highly evolved beings came to Earth to assist those incarnating on your planet with their spiritual growth and development. They came with the knowledge of how to function multidimensionally. All life throughout the many universes of the Creator knows at a primal level that it is moving inexorably back to union with the God Force or Ultimate Source of Energy. This is why there is a powerful, unremitting drive in every being, no matter how high or low, to evolve onto a more advanced level of manifestation.

The first souls who came onto the Earth plane had the capability of moving at will into other dimensions. It was as natural for them as it is for our readers to get into a car and travel to a new location. They could move in their astral bodies throughout the many galaxies and beyond. Or they could dissemble their physical bodies and reassemble them in a new location at will. What many of the beings who came to Earth lacked, however, was the knowledge of how to access the higher dimensions while existing within a dense gravitational pull.

And so it was that they had to immerse themselves in the Earth's gravity field for an extended period until they had internalized all levels of experience into their soul knowing. Once that task was accomplished, it was the intent of the spiritual blueprint that humanity would move upward into multidimensional functioning and join the many inhabitants of the higher realms as true participants in the divine dance of life.

Earth's inhabitants are on the brink of a great step forward. It will take many years for humanity as a whole to accomplish this goal. It is important for the spiritual pioneers on your planet to recognize that the process is starting and that they are meant to be the forerunners of a new type of human, one who can access higher dimensions at will for soul expansion and growth.

# Expanding Brain Capacity

We cannot emphasize strongly enough how important access-ing other dimensions is for the inhabitants of Earth. As more and more people on your planet experience those planes above the third dimension, their brains will expand into a more complex mental state – one that will allow them to think, compute, intuit and see in broader terms the realities of life all about them.

The most important step human beings on Earth are taking at the present time is the expansion of their mental faculties. This is the reason such emphasis has been placed on developing the left hemisphere of the brain in schools all over your planet. Both hemispheres of the brain must be activated and working in tan-dem with each other in order to access the higher dimensions. Prior to the age of reason and science the past three hundred years, the left hemisphere of the brain was underdeveloped and not ready for the advance humanity was scheduled to make in the twenty-first century.

It was intended from the outset of creation that human beings would use the total capacity of their brains. But as souls sunk ever deeper into the dense gravitational field of the Earth plane, the brain's ability to function at this more advanced level diminished. Humans lost their wondrous powers along with their higher mental and spiritual capabilities, which had been their birthright; but this loss was in keeping with the Divine Plan of the Creator. One cannot truly appreciate what it is to have a fully activated brain until that function has been lost and then found again. That is what the Divine Plan is all about – a mystery to be solved through experience and hard work on behalf of the soul.

Now that human beings on the Earth plane have increased their mental abilities, they are ready for a great expansion in brain capacity to occur. This step upward will be facilitated exponentially by multidimensional travel, because new pathways in the brain are created when one is exposed to an experience beyond what is known and believed to be possible. As the soul moves into the fourth dimension and experiences time as the Now where everything is occurring simultaneously, the idea of past, present and future becomes obsolete.

In order to grasp the new reality, nerve pathways in the brain are activated and expanded. The brain capacity is automatically enlarged, and light-encoded information circulates throughout parts of the brain that have been unused for eons. The brain simply cannot reflect a new reality without expanding so that it can register that reality. For this reason, Earth souls who enter a higher dimension are helping to birth a more advanced species of human being, one with greatly expanded personal powers and increased ability to connect with the Source of All That Is.

## The Many Dimensions of Heaven

The fourth dimension is a realm existing in close proximity to the third dimension of Earth. You may be surprised to hear that the fourth dimension is nearby, as you would say in your language. Nearby means that something is very close, and that is true for the fourth dimension. Many human beings have the concept that heaven is a far and distant place, difficult to find and hard to enter. This is a flawed view of heaven, one that has been in existence for some time.

All the dimensions higher than the one a person inhabits constitute what is called heaven. For heaven is a non-physical state of consciousness containing many different vibratory planes. These dimensions, as many call them, graduate from denser molecular fields to ones that are ever more refined in spiritual essence. The symbol that most accurately describes the many levels of spirit is the spiral, that ancient glyph found all over the Earth in the drawings of your ancestors.

These early people understood that the soul progresses upward through all the dimensions of time and space, constantly expanding consciousness and awareness on its journey back to reunion with the Creator. They also knew from experience that other dimensions interacted with their own in a direct and concrete way. Their lives and rituals emphasized the steps needed to access the spiritual realms, which they knew were just a heartbeat away. They carried this deep intuitive knowledge within them throughout their lives, using it as a guiding principle for their beliefs and behavior.

As the incarnating souls on Earth in the twenty-first century start to return to the knowledge base of their early ancestors, they will reintroduce interdimensional travel into the spiritual practices of many. The growth of meditation in the Western world has been the primary factor for this important step of spiritual development. Whereas prayer is the active outward communication with spirit, meditation is an inward process leading to connection with one's soul essence.

Many of the realms existing above the third dimension are entered by experiencing them at a soul level only. This is why adding meditation to one's spiritual practice is of such importance now. The physical vehicle will eventually accompany the soul as an integral unit when it ascends to the higher realms. But first the soul essence must be able to make the journey unencumbered.

For this reason, we urge the inhabitants of Earth to commit to a regular practice of meditation each day, if only for ten or fifteen minutes. The connection to one's soul wisdom provides the impetus needed for growth and development at all levels. Think of meditation as an uplifting spiritual practice, for that is what it truly is – your connection to the God Force, the greatest power for good in the universe.

There are many levels or dimensions that the human eye is not able to see at this point in time. Because they cannot be seen, however, does not mean that they do not exist. There are worlds beyond worlds reflecting, refracting and mingling throughout time and space. Those now living on the Earth plane cannot begin to imagine the myriad of life forms that can be found in the many universes of the Creator.

It always has been thus since the beginning of time. It was the intent of the Creator to provide a variety of life experiences so that all souls could grow and develop in a rich and ever-changing diversity of environments. Throughout the many universes and their galaxies, there are star systems and planets with a wide variety of life forms. Some of these are of a subtler level, having a higher and faster vibration that cannot condense into a physical body of human-like proportions.

The primary purpose of the Divine Creator always has been to provide a rich tapestry of experiences offering many opportunities so that the soul can grow and ascend into a final mastery of all planes and dimensions. This statement contains in its entirety the true meaning of existence. Each of us, as an essence of Divine Oneness, has one and only one goal. Our task is to flow through the many universes of time and space experiencing every aspect of life before we finally merge with the God Force. Once we have accomplished this, we become co-creators with a deep awareness of what that term truly means.

Why are we speaking about a concept that appears to be so esoteric and far removed from everyday life? We do so because this fundamental truth is the cornerstone of life and needs to be recognized as the basic premise for all that we are. If one perceives the purpose of existence as the gathering of knowledge and experience to gain mastery, every event is seen as ultimately uplifting in nature. If one does not succeed in a certain area, it is best viewed as part of a long and exciting adventure culminating in ultimate reunion with the Creator.

The educational process always contains within it the necessity for trial and error. When one needs to go back over a life lesson a few times to really incorporate it into soul knowing, it is never viewed at a higher level as failure. It is only an act of refining something that is important in the development of the soul. When human beings incorporate this simple but profound concept into the true meaning of existence, it will change the manner in which they see themselves and their lives. The idea of failure would be totally eradicated from human perception and would be replaced by the realization that everything gained through experience contributes to ultimate perfection.

Our readers may ask if our information will be relevant to most people. We can only assure you that a higher purpose is unfolding here. Our words will strike a deep chord in the minds and hearts of many. Also, spiritual imprints long held by those currently incarnating on Earth will be activated by reading our words. The essence of this book contains an energy field that will elevate the consciousness of its readers, raising them to a higher level of human awareness.

# Quantum Physics – A New Picture of Reality

All life throughout the many universes of time and space is participating in a divine dance of the Creator. As science continues to probe the reality of life, the teachings of mystics and sages down through the ages will be proven in a direct way. Each time humanity takes a step up the spiral of life, a new scientific theory appears to anchor in third-dimensional thought the spiritual truths needed for increased human awareness.

Quantum physics is the latest in a long line of scientific theories that have appeared at key times to explain spiritual truths. Quantum theory is revolutionary in its premise. It presents a new picture of reality that expands the boundaries of knowledge concerning the nature of life. As scientists are able to distill the complexity of the theory into layman's language, it will be disseminated to the public through educational institutions and the media in ever widening circles. Gradually, the truths of this new line of scientific thought will form the cornerstone of humanity's view of its physical and spiritual world.

In simplified terms, quantum theory says that life exists in an energetic field that is always changing and transforming according to the stimuli being applied to that field at any given time. Therefore, reality as we know it is not as it appears to humans immersed in the belief system of the current age. When one looks at a table, one sees a solid object, when in reality the table is comprised of minute particles called quanta that are swimming in a field of space.

As human beings develop an increased ability to see the true makeup of matter, both manmade and natural, they will recognize that they exist in a field of subatomic particles. These particles flow and change as the mind force of those observing them impacts them. So the idea that reality is a static constant is erroneous and must be dropped from the knowledge base of human beings residing on Earth.

As this new theory gains acceptance, it will provide a launching pad for interdimensional travel. Incarnating souls on Earth will learn that they are energy fields operating within a greater energy field, which changes as they bring consciousness to it. As humans experiment with their growing ability to change their physical world, they will be catapulted into new and complex realities. They will initiate travel to ever more exquisitely subtle and refined levels of existence. In doing so, they will expand the awareness of what it means to be a soul living within a physical body that has the ability to access many different kinds of reality at will.

## Time's Shift into a New Paradigm

Humans on your planet are becoming aware that time is changing and shifting into a new paradigm. Have you not heard many people say time seems to be moving much faster than in earlier years? And this is actually what is happening. The acceleration of time is occurring all over the Earth. As events speed up, it is as if time were folding back on itself, bringing to the surface issues and circumstances people have already experienced in order for them to be addressed again.

This modification in time gives the inhabitants of your planet an opportunity to review any longstanding issues needing resolution. For humanity to take a great step forward on its spiritual journey, it must resolve anything that might be an impediment to soul growth. Therefore, time on the one hand appears to be accelerating while it also seems to be retrograding back to earlier events, which have not been totally reconciled or healed.

The truth is that time consists of past, present and future all occurring in the ever-present Now. More people will be experiencing past and present simultaneously as they move into each new moment of the future. Little do they realize that they are, in effect, getting a preview of the principal characteristic of the vibratory field of the fourth dimension.

We are speaking of this subject now so that our readers can reflect upon what we say. This is an important concept for you to incorporate into your soul knowing. And so, if former painful circumstances and actions that you thought were resolved are surfacing in your life once again, accept them with gratitude. They are offering you an opening into the reality of the fourth dimension, if you choose to take it. The choice is up to you!

# The Twenty-first Century and Beyond

We would like to speak now about the coming times, a subject that is of great interest to the inhabitants of your planet. By the beginning years of the twenty-first century, it became evident to most people that extremely negative events were growing in magnitude and force. It seemed that people's lives were escalating out of control, causing deep anxiety and uncertainty for those souls living on Earth during this period. We would like to reassure our readers that all is in Divine Order and perfect in the higher scheme of things.

For as we have said, a great cleansing is occurring, which will prepare the Earth for a new phase of human development. Think of the beauty of the rainbow that comes after the storm, touching its viewers with awe and wonder while they gaze at the marvel displayed in the heavens. As the arc of brilliant colors spreads across the sky, those watching often feel a sense of connection with something greater than themselves. A rainbow has long been a gift from God expressing the love and promise that all is well.

We ask our readers to carry the sign of the rainbow in your hearts as you move through the years ahead. Know that the love of the Creator is always supporting and uplifting you in the most trying of times. You will never be abandoned by those on the realm of spirit who have always been there for you, even though you might not know of their presence. Your universe is an interactive and interconnected matrix of existence. No section or part of it is removed or isolated from the love of its Creator.

Your soul knows that you are never alone. So we ask that you incorporate that knowing into your human consciousness. Move forward with courage and grace into these challenging times, which have been anticipated and prepared for by the ancient ones on your planet for many eons. Inhabitants of Earth are entering the period of the Great Awakening. The seemingly destructive events in your world are simply removing the darkness and dross of many centuries of existence.

Your beautiful blue-green planet, which has long served as a laboratory for the spiritualization of matter, is about to be irradiated with powerful vibrations from the center of your galaxy. All life on your planet will be forever changed as a great step up the spiral of life occurs. Open yourselves up to the blessed rays of your Creator. You are loved far beyond what you can envision, child of the universe. You have our honor and respect for all that you are and all that you will be!

In the first hundred years of the twenty-first century, the pattern will be set for the nine hundred years to follow. It is ever thus that the prototype is established at the outset of any endeavor and serves as the guiding principle for the entire period. With this overriding truth in mind, we ask our readers to recognize the significance of the years that are unfolding in this new century.

From the years 2001 through 2100, the archetypal overlay for the millennium will be put in place. Therefore it is essential that all those living in this seminal time see the importance of the task they agreed to do when they incarnated on the Earth plane. They were to honor the creative significance of this period and consciously involve themselves in the great planetary event, which is unfolding. Each and every person living on the Earth now has come to contribute in some particular manner to the creation of a new age. There is a deep soul knowing as to how this personal offering will manifest.

This is why so many individuals possess both a sense of urgency and a feeling of personal mission. Many times, the purpose has not been identified; but there is awareness of something important the individual must do that will contribute to the greater good. It is also intuitively known that the life mission should be identified and embarked upon as soon as possible.

## A New Age in Human Development

The reason a portion of this book has been devoted to interdimensional travel is that a large segment of the human race will be participating in this type of travel during the next two hundred years. Those who are pioneering this endeavor are serving as progenitors of a new species of human being who will emerge in the coming years to populate the Earth.

Down through the eons, the human species has experienced numerous turns on the spiral of life. Each turn has brought expanded capabilities and characteristics that have been incorporated into the genetic code and have become part of the human DNA. The perfect prototype for all human beings lived in the earliest days on the planet, serving as a model and coexisting with the animal life that appeared at that time.

Up to the present day, there has been no proof available to substantiate this statement. Every major age has ended in a catastrophe of worldwide proportions. Fire, wind, flood and comets colliding with the Earth have destroyed almost all life except for a few isolated remnants. Each time, the signs of human existence have been obliterated. The few telltale indications of early human habitation lie buried deep within the soil of the Earth, to be discovered only if the higher powers deem it necessary for the evolutionary knowledge of the human race.

The end of a great twenty-six-thousand-year cycle is fast approaching. There will be an event of planetary significance occurring within the next one hundred years that will mark the end of this long period of time and the beginning of a new age in humankind's development. What this event will be and how it will manifest is still in the formative stage. The Four Primary Forces will determine the appropriate time and circumstances for this occurrence. At the beginning of time, the Creator gave these Forces the responsibility for generating the power needed to activate all life in the universe. Therefore, they will provide the force required to initiate this process.

However, the actions of the people of Earth can play a significant role in impacting the severity and quality of the change. All life is in a constant state of flux, continuously moving and shifting. This is why prophecy must be viewed as a description of probable futures that may or may not occur. Every being possesses the God-given right of free will to modify and change future events, even those of planetary significance.

This truth regarding freedom of choice explains why prophecy is so important. It provides a window into the possibility of future happenings. People can change their future and create a totally different outcome by their commitment and intent. Anything is possible in the many universes of the Creator. You have the power to formulate a future that is positive in every respect. All it requires is that you hold your vision true and steady. By so doing you can create your future reality exactly as you wish it to be.

As human beings attune to spirit through meditation, prayer and contemplation, they will change physically, emotionally, psychologically and spiritually. It is increasingly important that this process is understood. One cannot be in constant contact with a higher energy source for an extended period without significant changes occurring at all levels of the being. Physically, the body becomes stronger and healthier. Illness becomes a rarity, appearing more as release of old karmic patterns and situations than sickness caused by the current life.

Whether one is aware of it or not, the actual physical structure of the body is transformed. If one accesses many different sources of healing, the body's endocrine glands rejuvenate and clear themselves. Restorative forces from the realm of spirit are of assistance many times without one being conscious of them. In addition, continuous meditation over an extended period activates the body at a cellular level, renewing all bodily functions.

As more humans work on emotional healing, it will have a profound affect upon them. The depth of the healing extends into the personal memory bank located adjacent to the spinal column in the energy body surrounding the physical form. Every soul in or out of incarnation possesses this memory bank, which contains the knowledge of all accumulated experience. As a soul heals emotionally, the content of the memory bank is restructured, which assists the soul in ascending to a higher form of existence.

While one heals emotionally, the psychological state improves and elevates, which in turn affects one's worldview in profound ways. The changes that occur shift paradigms and directly impact one's behavior, creating major personality realignment, closer to the true soul essence. As one heals and expands physically, emotionally and psychologically, the soul essence receives the benefit of more powerful spiritual energy emanations, which bring increased molecules of light to all levels of the being. So you see, each soul ascends up the spiral of life by doing the work essential to spiritual advancement, no matter where or in what context the growth occurs.

## The Great Purification

In 2005, a new paradigm began to unfold in the United States and throughout the world. The intensity of the Great Purification, long prophesied by the indigenous cultures in the Americas and throughout the Earth, began in earnest. The second decade of the twenty-first century will be one of great turmoil and strife. The people of Earth will be experiencing the birth pangs of a New World, which will be very different in many ways. In order for the inhabitants of your planet to evolve onto a higher level, certain basic beliefs and practices must be modified and changed. First and foremost, they must realize at a deep level of soul knowing that they are spiritual beings currently inhabiting a physical form in order to grow and expand.

They also need to know that they are interconnected with all that exists. For every soul is connected in ever expanding concentric circles of existence to the Creator of All That Is. Because of this connection, each soul has access to the ultimate source of power. This power is to be used for the purpose of manifesting whatever creates the highest good throughout time and space. We ask that you reflect upon what we have just said.

Think of what a different world your Earth would be if all of its people were committed to manifesting the highest good in every situation. War, anger, hatred, greed and all the other hurtful dynamics of human interaction would be eliminated, since they are never an expression of the highest good. When one realizes that he or she is directly connected to everything that exists, it soon becomes impossible to interact in a damaging manner with anyone else. How can a soldier kill another soldier when he knows he is killing a part of himself?

This knowledge of spiritual connection to all that exists is paradigm changing at the deepest level. Until this realization is widespread, the dynamics of the Old World will continue. This is why the people of Earth are going through the agonies of war, conflict and hatred. These agonies are grist for the mill. They are the forces bringing purification and change. Just as the beautiful pearl is formed through the corrosive action of the sand within its shell, so the inhabitants of your planet need to experience pain and suffering to rise to a higher realm. On your planet, there is no other way for evolution of consciousness to occur.

Therefore, the escalation in conflict is leading to the final realization that war and strife can never be a part of human interaction. Incarnating souls have to reach that place where they commit to living with each other from a position of love and respect in all circumstances. This is why the affairs of humans are escalating in a crescendo of pain and fear. Ultimately the people of Earth will be forced by the extreme negativity of their lives to make the fundamental choice for what creates the highest good. When all souls develop that realization as a conscious knowing, a New World will start to emerge on planet Earth!

## The Secret of Eternal Life

There is a significant issue that needs to be addressed by the people of Earth as they move into the coming age. It is the concept of immortality as it is presently conceived by humanity. Down through the ages, there has been a search for the secret to life that does not end with death. Humans always have been fascinated with the possibility of living forever. Many individuals in the past have spent their entire lives searching for the key to this mystery.

And a mystery it truly is! The secret of eternal life has beckoned like a flame in the minds of those living on your planet. Since inhabitants of the Earth are residing on the third-dimensional plane, the view of immortality is very limited as it relates to the reality of living forever. The idea has taken hold because of humanity's lack of understanding about the true concept of life.

In the earliest days of intelligent habitation on the planet, incarnating souls understood fully what it was to live forever. They knew that they were a form of spiritual energy, which could never be destroyed. Energy, once created, lives forever. It might change, but it never can be nullified or exterminated in any fashion. With this knowledge at the core of their being, souls reentered your beautiful planet over and over to gain experience on their return to the Source.

Each time, they took on a new persona that would help them grow and develop on this plane. They understood that the personality they adopted for a short time was perfect in all ways for their ongoing spiritual journey. They knew that the physical body was a temporary sheath enclosing the glory of their eternal soul. They also were aware, at the core of their being, that their consciousness would never die but would continue on forever, albeit in varying forms and essences.

So it is that the truth regarding immortality has existed since the beginning of time. The search for it symbolizes human beings' loss of awareness about the reality of who they are and from whence they have come. Many have mistakenly thought that the discovery of physical immortality was their goal and have pursued the means to prolong life, when in actuality they were trying to rediscover their true divinity.

One of the most significant developments in the next two centuries will be the worldwide realization concerning the everlasting life of the soul. When the majority of humanity knows that they have an immortal soul, which possesses eternal life, a higher level of consciousness will have been reached. There will be a blossoming of untold magnitude. Each person will understand his or her true role in relation to self, others, the planet and the universe. Then, and only then, will a new heaven and a new Earth emerge, allowing humanity to rise on the spiral of life.

## Humanity's Spiritual Blueprint

The hunger for spiritual knowledge is growing exponentially on your planet. Intuitively people know that they must expand

and seek a new paradigm, because life is currently empty and without meaning for many. When one reaches this juncture, there is a much greater willingness to explore new avenues of thought. Many inhabitants on Earth know that they are living in extraordinary times. They recognize their world is rapidly changing in a tumultuous way. Most think the change is occurring on the outer plane and do not recognize what vast changes are happening first on the inner plane of spirit. For, as we have said before, all that manifests in the physical world originates from the plane of Pure Idea. When intent arises, it forms a blueprint for what is to be created. Then, and only then, can something appear physically.

Incarnating souls on your planet must recognize that there is a spiritual blueprint in place for humanity, which is about to take an evolutionary step up the spiral of life. In order for this to happen, much of the old must be swept away in preparation for a new paradigm to unfold. Therefore, cultures, governments, ways of life and the land itself will change to reflect the needs of the new emerging human species. You may ask, why does the land have to change for this evolutionary step to occur?

Physical location and geographical characteristics are highly significant in the development of a people and their culture. Think of how significant the North American continent was to the development of the United States and Canada. Their physical isolation, with the protection of large oceans on their eastern and western shores, afforded them the opportunity to develop without having to fight conquering armies at their borders. Their vast size also was a protective factor assisting in the unbroken growth and expansion of these two great nations.

Climate, hemispheric location and relationship to neighboring people also play a major role in the history of any culture.

Therefore, as the blueprint is being formed on the level of spirit for the creation of a new civilization for humans, careful consideration is being given to the land the people will inhabit. Does it offer a suitable environment for the experiences this culture will encounter? Every significant civilization has been located on a continent that supported and enhanced the life lessons needed by the souls incarnating within that matrix.

So it is that as new civilizations emerge, they require an appropriate physical environment. What this means is that the landmasses of today must be altered to facilitate the next evolutionary step. A great deal has been written in recent years about coming Earth changes. This information has emerged to help humans prepare for the alterations that will occur in their physical environment.

Mother Earth is a self-renewing and recirculating system governed by a high level of intelligence. Periodically, she modifies her physical structure so that the human beings on her surface can participate in a new series of life experiences. She is about to embark upon another alteration in the configuration of her landmasses. As this proceeds over the next two centuries, the maps charting land on your planet will change. Two hundred years from now, people will be living on land not yet formed, and some populous areas will no longer be in existence.

## Major Themes for the New Millennium

The opening decade of the twenty-first century is meant to be a time of trial and testing for all inhabitants of Earth in a wide variety of ways. This century is a birthing time for this new millennium and contains all the elements of the next one thousand years in microcosmic form. The issues humans will face in the first one hundred years will serve as a template for the remaining nine hundred years. At the end of the twenty-first century, the major themes for the millennium will have been put in place energetically. As our readers can see, this current period is pivotal in the affairs of souls incarnating on the Earth. You are part of a creative process that is establishing the blueprint for this millennium.

What will be the themes for the thousand-year period that has just begun? There are three that will surface continuously through these years in varying circumstances. The first is the issue of love for the Earth with all of her many diverse life forms. The prevailing wisdom of indigenous tribes throughout your planet recognizes her spiritual essence and honors her for the gift of life she has given those who live on her surface. This love for and connection to the Great Mother must become an underlying tenet for all people. When incarnating souls acknowledge their responsibility toward Mother Earth and become dedicated to her in a harmonious and supportive way, a major point in the spiritual growth of the planet and her people will have been reached.

The second theme will be the need for love of one's fellow humans, as well as all life forms existing on the planet. In order to reach this state of unconditional love, certain behavior and acts will have to cease. The issues of anger, hatred, warfare, and greed need to be faced and eradicated from the human condition. For many eons, these detriments to spiritual progress have surfaced over and over again. Ever so slowly, however, the inhabitants of Earth are starting to see more clearly the harm these conditions cause. There is a growing recognition that a positive way must be found for interacting with each other. As incarnating souls on Earth attune directly to their soul wisdom, the dark energies spawning hurtful actions toward others will dissipate and be removed from your planet.

The third theme of the next one thousand years will be the increasing abilities of Earth's inhabitants to access higher dimensions of time and space. At the end of the next one thousand years, the inhabitants of your planet will have become multi-dimensional travelers and citizens of the galaxy. In the future, Earth beings will venture out into the farthest reaches of space, exploring and seeding future worlds, beyond the knowledge of science at the present time. Travel, however, will not be limited to outer space alone. Humans will gain the ability to go within and access higher dimensions of reality in a wide variety of ways. Their expanded brain capacities and spiritual capabilities will provide the launching pad for inner exploration. The twenty-first century will set the tone for these extraordinary events. Are you not fortunate to be living in such a wondrous and creative time?

## A Time of Awakening

There are many realms and planes of existence within the universes of time and space. These dimensions hold a myriad of experiences for the soul on its journey back to the God Force. Throughout the eons, it has been the pattern of the soul to move into and immerse itself in the diverse worlds that proliferate the cosmos. The prevalent view in the current third-dimensional realm of Earth is that the reality of the physical plane is all that exists. Nothing could be farther from the truth.

The new millennium will see the end of this limited perception of life. It was perfect in the divine scheme that the focus for those living on the Earth was purely third-dimensional. Immersion in the world of matter was part of the intended pattern for humanity. A complete grounding in the forces of physical matter has to occur before the spiritualizing process can begin.

The archetypal pattern for the divine drama of the Earth's universe is one of involution and evolution. The individual sparks of spirit sent out by the Creator have a definite task to perform. They are to enter all types of situations to gain knowledge, depth and wisdom. Once this has been accomplished over many eons, the souls begin the journey home, fully ready to join as co-creators with the God Force. Simply stated – spirit moves ever deeper into matter, reaching the point of maximum density. Then the return begins with spirit conjoining matter, ultimately to achieve a divine union of cosmic proportions.

The information we have just provided the reader is life transforming in all ways. It gives a totally different comprehension for the troubling issues of these times – war, famine, death, and corruption. So often the question is asked, "Why is all this pain a part of the human condition?" The answer is beautiful in its simplicity. The children of God are experiencing the depth of negativity in order to gain love, wisdom and compassion. There is no other way than to undergo the suffering necessary to develop these fruits of the spirit.

If every person residing on the Earth could realize the meaning inherent in the traumas of life, the cause for suffering would be raised to a higher level of understanding. There would be a strength and ability to cope with the adversities that impact everyone. An expanded comprehension regarding the necessity for such painful travail uplifts the individual and makes everything easier to endure. We ask our readers to reflect on our words. The truth of what we say will raise you up on eagle's wings to soar into the higher realms of the Creator free and unencumbered at last!

There is a growing awareness that much exists beyond what we can perceive on the third-dimensional plane. Intuitive and psychic abilities are increasing within a larger portion of the populace on Earth. Many are seeing beings from other realms as well as those who reside in other parts of the galaxy and universe. Contact with loved ones who passed on is becoming far more common. Even technology is assisting in the expanding capabilities of humans. Beings from the higher realms are now communicating through the radio, TV, computer and, in rare cases, the telephone. A greater percentage of people in the United States have had direct contact with non-Earth beings at some time in their lives.

But generally these instances have been identified as unusual peak experiences, a rare instance in the normal course of affairs. There is very little awareness on the part of humans as to how easily these realms can be accessed. Because they do not yet recognize the higher dimensional activities occurring on overlapping planes of existence, they are missing the rich tapestry of life being woven all about them. Examples of this phenomenon are the sense of seeing something out of the corner of one's eye or the gut level feeling that something is nearby that cannot be seen.

If the people of Earth could see what really is happening on different but interactive dimensions, they would be shaken to the core. The world is teeming with life forms of every conceivable size, shape and color. These forms are growing, moving, experiencing and dying in an ever-circling wave of activity that gives beauty and depth to the concept of the divine creation.

There are a few people on the Earth that have the ability to see these other realms of existence. The pathways of their brain have been rewired into a new configuration that provides an expanded sense of sight. They interact and participate in the world of these other realms most often in a contemplative or sleep state. It is the rare being, indeed, who can participate simultaneously in two or more parallel happenings on different realms at the same time.

However, it will be a common occurrence for the new species that will reside on the Earth in future times. Their expanded brains will be capable of instantaneous contact with any source they choose within the galaxy. They will be able to exist in third-dimensional form in more than one locale at the same time. Also, they will be able to project an image of themselves holographically to any place they designate in the universe.

The time of purification that the native peoples have long heralded is now at hand. An extensive cycle of time has drawn to a close, and a new spiral of unfolding is about to begin. One of the primary characteristics of this new cycle will be the emergence of a new prototype of human being to play out the human drama, which began in earnest over a million years ago.

The people who have lived on your beautiful planet, strategically located in a key area of the Milky Way Galaxy, have experienced much. For Earth was designated in the beginning days of this life cycle to play a role of major significance in the enactment of the Divine Plan. She was formed to be one of the laboratories of creation where the merging of spirit and matter would occur. In this cauldron of continuing transformation, spirit would experience the density of matter. Slowly and inexorably, matter would be transmuted, illuminated and expanded until a divine union of the positive and negative poles of reality would blend and harmonize into a symphony of the spheres.

One of the most significant developments to occur in the next twenty to fifty years will be the recognition by all humans that they are part of a universe teeming with life forms of all types and varieties. The growing interest in the phenomenon of UFOs represents, at a deeper level, a readiness on the part of Earth inhabitants to acknowledge that they are only one of many life forms existing in every sector of the universe.

Many of the earlier cultures knew the Star People, as they were generally called, and interacted with them in countless ways. This contact gave them a much more expanded view of themselves and the world in which they lived. It also allowed them to activate personal powers that have since lain dormant in the psyche and genetic matrix of later Earth inhabitants.

But humanity is like the princess in the fairy tale of the sleeping beauty. Many people are awakening and seeing their world in a new and more realistic way. They are developing a deep, intuitive knowing that they are not alone. They also know that they are spirit beings, encased in a physical form, playing out a divine drama of cosmic proportions. To see life in this manner is to expand human awareness in a leap of quantum proportions, which will crack the genetic code and send human beings off to a more highly developed level on the spiral of life.

## The Gathering Storm

The summer of 2004 will be looked upon by many as the calm before the storm. Those of us on the realm of spirit possess a higher vantage point for viewing the affairs of humans on Earth. We are able to see past, present and future with a clarity and unity that is not possible for those living on your planet. Just as meteorologists have satellites that give them a picture seen from the higher reaches of space, we can observe what is unfolding through a clear and expanded lens.

For this reason, we can alert our readers to the turbulent times ahead. There is a great advantage to knowing that a storm of serious proportions is bearing down on you, whether you are on land or sea. One can prepare and make choices that will alleviate the impact of the storm to some degree. What we are presenting to you is a spiritual weather map, in some respects. For even though the coming events will be appearing in your lives as everyday occurrences, they are developing from a spiritual blueprint created to raise humanity to a higher, more refined level of consciousness.

One of the most important preparations one can make is to hold true to the knowing that what is coming is for the highest good. We ask our readers to start to think of yourselves as if you were residents of the Caribbean and knew that a major hurricane was about to hit your island. What is generally done under these circumstances? Some people choose to evacuate and relocate in a safer locale, either temporarily or permanently. Others stay where they are and try to protect their homes and property to the best of their ability. They stock up on basic essentials and attempt to ride out the storm.

These choices are very similar to those that will be made by people all over the Earth who live where strife, conflict and natural disasters continue to escalate with ever-stronger intensity. Warfare will increase as the polarizing factions in the Eastern and Western worlds strive for supremacy over their opponents. For Christians, it will appear that Armageddon is here; and in some respects that is an accurate perception. Humans of the future will recognize the days ahead as a defining moment in the spiritual growth and development for the people of Earth.

The issue of paramount significance here is the evolutionary need for humanity to move through duality into unity. The secondary question to be addressed is whether the people of Earth can stop the use of warfare as a means of solving disputes and settling differences. The pain and suffering the people of your planet have experienced down through the ages because of war and conflict must stop. Not only is the very fabric of civilization unraveling, but Mother Earth herself has been seriously weakened by the ongoing wars of the twentieth and twenty-first centuries. Can you not feel her travail? The natural disasters of ever-increasing magnitude are a true reflection of her suffering. Wake up, people of Earth. You are seriously harming the mother who has given you the very land on which you live.

## Earth Changes

It now is time to consider the changes that are going to occur on the Earth in the coming decades and centuries. We ask you to take a deep breath and let go of all judgment. What will appear has been set in motion within the great cycle of life and can be modified to some degree but not completely changed. For there is a rhythm and intent to the plan of the Creator, which unfolds in a beautiful and synchronistic way, always working for the highest good.

All creation is in the process of evolving to the highest expression possible, no matter how simple or complex the level of development. As these forms of matter proceed up the spiral of their evolutionary development, they are involved in a dance of cosmic proportions. Transmuting to an ever-higher form requires a perpetual impetus for ascension to greater knowledge and experience. This defines the energy dynamic of evolution –

a never-ending instinct for rising to a more complex form of development. In order for intelligent life on the many planets of your universe to ascend up this spiral of life, a matrix envisioned from a spiritual blueprint must exist on the plane where the unfolding is taking place.

The spiritual blueprint for the Earth was simple in its intent. Your planet was meant to serve as a laboratory where spirit and matter could exhibit the beauty of union – that state where opposites come together in harmony and love, exemplifying the highest expression of the Godhead's essence. And so it has been that different cultures have lived upon your planet, contributing to the unification of spirit and matter. They have evolved in environments where opposition and polarity were paramount, but always manifesting a different set of circumstances for each individual culture.

The civilizations existing on the Earth have needed physical locales complementary to their life experiences. The new human species starting to appear on your planet needs to occupy land that is not tainted with the vibrations of earlier peoples. This is the primary reason why landmasses must shift and change in the coming years. Mother Earth recycles her available land to provide the best possible soil for human development, just as a farmer allows some land to lie fallow, rotating it until it is most advantageous for the growth of a certain crop.

It is now time for certain lands on your planet to lie fallow, resting while they await the appearance of future civilizations. The reconfiguration of landmasses will cause your planet's terrain to go through many changes in the next two hundred years. Climatic conditions will bring changes that will force people to move to safer locales. Severe earthquakes, tornadoes and storms of increasing magnitude, as well as the shifting of the Earth's crust, will cause the sinking of some lands and the rising of others. You must be wondering what the people of Earth can do during the turmoil these changes will cause.

There are specific things that incarnating souls can do as they struggle with the events coming into their lives. In our first book, *Dreaming a New World,* we offered some suggestions, which we would like to repeat here exactly as we stated them, since they still have great significance.

In looking at the question of how one can prepare for the coming Earth changes, the first decision that has to be made is whether one wants to do anything at all. Every person alive during this period has requested to be here and has a specific idea of what he or she is to do. But the attraction of third-dimensional matter can pull one away from the intent of spirit, resulting in a rejection of that earlier commitment. The Creator has given each soul free will and the right to exercise it at any given point in time.

For those who wish to ride the wave of this evolutionary step forward, we have this to say to you. Believe at a deep level of being that these changes are coming. First and foremost, prepare yourselves physically, emotionally, psychologically, and spiritually in whatever ways you see best, so that you are operating at peak effectiveness when the changes occur. Secondly, learn how to take care of your basic needs for food, clothing, shelter, and medicine. Thirdly, attune yourself to spirit and be certain that you are residing in a geographic location that will sustain you on all levels. Fourthly, insure that there are people living near you who can serve as a support network for you in time of need.

Finally, develop a vision of yourself living in a state of well being during the times of greatest crisis. Hold this positive vision as you go about preparing yourself on a mundane level for what is to come. Always keep in mind that a new freshness of the land

and a rainbow of hope for the future will come after a storm of any duration. All of these events will have washed away the Old World and ushered in a new Heaven and a new Earth that has been spoken about for many centuries in the past.

There also are personal traits that will be essential in the years to come. They are openness, receptivity to inner prompting, flexibility, and courage to follow one's own convictions. It will be necessary to look with joy and understanding at the events that are unfolding. Think of the birth process. It is painful and chaotic but totally worth it in all ways. A New World is being born, and those experiencing it are the pioneers of the coming age. What an honor indeed! Step forward with courage and confidence no matter what transpires. All is in divine order, and each and every one of you is loved and appreciated.

The months and years that lie ahead are of profound significance for the souls incarnating on your planet. The analogy of the hurricane depicts most clearly what is unfolding on Mother Earth at the present time. Using the example of the hurricane, a powerful storm of varying degrees of intensity, is useful since the extent and magnitude of these acts of nature will continue to increase throughout the decades to come.

Let us discuss for a moment the nature of hurricanes and how they manifest. A hurricane is a vortex of swirling circular energy that begins its formation over large bodies of water as differing atmospheric wind patterns come together. The radiating circular form that a hurricane develops is found in all nature from the smallest droplet of water to the largest galaxy in the universe. A deeper understanding of the creative process can be found by observing the swirling air mass of a hurricane.

A hurricane is atmospheric energy radiating out in ever-larger concentric circles from a seemingly empty center. And yet these powerful storms are created from this space, which is calm, peaceful and quiet. The question is often asked, "How can such a violent and powerful storm be formed from a center that is its opposite in every way?" Those who have flown through the ferocious buffeting winds of a major hurricane and entered its eye speak of the awe, wonder and deep peace experienced in this space.

Many have said that it was an intensely spiritual experience for them. At an intuitive level, often unknowingly, they were sensing a profound truth about the nature of the Source of Life. For all that exists is created by the Primal Force, which is unseen, unknown and unmanifested. Many forms of life radiate out from the circular center of the Source, which is why every thing found in all the universes of time and space reflects the essence of its Creator.

Observing hurricanes on television has become a common activity for those living on Earth. As many watch the formation and path of these great storms, their consciousness is being raised without their knowledge by pictures that contain a profound truth about the Creative Force. Even though they are unaware of it, they are being imprinted at the cellular level with a visual image that reflects back the true nature of God.

Using the hurricane as a focus for our words is significant for two reasons. First, hurricanes are gaining in power and force, bringing public attention to the nature and progress of these storms as never before. Second, the hurricane presents a visual picture that will serve as a spiritual symbol for those incarnating souls who will be coping with tumultuous events all over the Earth in the coming years.

Let us now consider the physical form of the hurricane. As this powerful vortex of energy comes into existence, it assumes a circular path that radiates as if it were moving around a clock. It increases or decreases in power and direction according to the properties of the atmospheric pressure in its surrounding vacinity. It causes great devastation from wind, rain, tornadoes and flooding when it moves over the land in its path.

The people caught in its wake experience deeply transformative life-changing events. Some miraculously escape the wrath of the storm, while others lose all that is near and dear to them. And thus it will be for those living on your planet. Some will ride out the years ahead with minimal effects upon them, while others will feel the full fury of events unfolding in their areas. Make no mistake; Mother Earth is moving into a period that will be one of the most challenging in the history of the planet.

We do not say these words to frighten or alarm you unnecessarily. We bring this information to alert you to the coming events, which will affect those living all over the Earth. We have said before; Mother Earth is going through an initiation of major proportions – as are the people living on her surface. This initiation will bring about an elevation in consciousness for the great soul infusing your planet, as well as for those who have come into incarnation to join her in reaching a higher level of spiritual development.

This process simulates giving birth, and therefore contains all the pain and travails experienced by a mother as she brings forth her unborn child. The difficult events of the coming years are but precursors to a more enlightened and spiritually uplifting time. We speak of these matters to prepare you for the challenges that will appear in your lives on many different levels.

We want to emphasize that every person living on the Earth today is capable of dealing with anything that comes into his or her life. Down through the eons you all have prepared for this crucial period in human development and offered to come and serve in the unfolding of the Divine Plan. You have the strength and fortitude to prevail no matter what unfolds in your lives. You are children of God working in the vineyards of the Creator. Never forget this truth! It will sustain you throughout the coming times.

We have offered you the picture of the hurricane as a symbol to hold in your hearts as you move forward in the coming years. Always remember that the powerful winds rotate around its center, which is calm, peaceful and quiet. You can achieve this same state as destructive forces escalate all about you. By going within through meditation, prayer, and contemplation, you can connect with your spiritual essence, which is a spark of the Divine Creator.

Once you open yourselves to experiencing the love of God, you will be able to face anything that occurs in your lives with equanimity, poise and the necessary strength of spirit. Also know that many beings on the realm of spirit are with you assisting in ways seen and unseen. There is a great abundance of love and support for all of you. You are blessed and honored for the roles you are playing in the long-awaited transformation of Mother Earth.

It is important that the people of Earth know the positions of the planets and various star systems in their galaxy. The ancients were aware that these bodies emitted vibratory rays of a specific spiritual quality, impacting them and their lives in a direct and powerful way. So they studied the paths of the heavenly bodies and reported on the significance of these movements to their people.

The ancient ones were able to predict political and sociological changes that would affect their people. By charting the stars, they were able to determine when their cultures would rise and fall. This knowledge allowed their rulers to prepare the people for what was to come. Most of all, it gave them the faith that a plan of spiritual importance was unfolding in an orderly and identifiable way. This comforting belief provided them the serenity they needed to accept what was occurring in their lives and move forward with a sense of well being, knowing that all was for the highest good.

Although the ancient study of the stars does not play an integral role in most societies on the Earth today, it still has as much relevance for the people of your planet as it did in earlier times. The heavenly bodies emit a specific type of spiritual energy, which contributes to the overall function of the galaxy itself. Therefore, it would be helpful to look at the impact that key star systems have on your planet in this day and age. By doing so, incarnating souls can recognize the order, beauty and perfection existing within every circumstance in their lives. The suffering accompanying painful changes in their lives can be seen as necessary for the unfolding of their higher purpose, as well as for that of the planet herself.

The Earth is moving into the very center of your galaxy and is entering an area that the ancients called the Womb of the Mother. This space is pregnant with powerful spiritual stimuli, which will initiate an evolutionary step forward of major proportions for all souls on your planet. Your solar system and other heavenly bodies are assisting Earth in this process as she ends a preparatory cycle of long duration. The spiritual energies of death and dissolution are being beamed to your planet in waves of increasingly powerful intensity. Much of the Old World needs to die as Mother Earth and her inhabitants prepare for the regeneration and rebirth that is about to occur.

And so we ask our readers to accept that the chaos you observe in your lives and your world has meaning beyond what you might be able to discern. Outdated ways of thinking and living must be discarded so that people with higher capabilities can step forward to have their time in the sun. Remember that the ancient Greeks viewed chaos as the condition that offered the greatest creativity and potential for growth. Walk forward into the times ahead with your heads held high and your hearts full of trust and love for the beauty of God's Plan. We are all truly blessed, are we not?

The gathering storm fast approaching your planet is made up of vibratory waves from worldwide conflict that will radiate out and eventually encompass the entire Earth in varying degrees of intensity. We know our words are distressing to you, and for that we are truly sorry. But reality must be faced and dealt with in the most positive way possible. It is important to always hold the knowledge that whatever is unfolding is always for the highest good. Know that the silver lining will shine through if one just transcends what is transpiring and sees it from a broader spiritual point of view.

You ask, how can the highest good emerge from suffering, grief and death? Painful circumstances hone the essence of the soul just as a forge refines the metal placed within its fire. Think of the people you know who have suffered great tragedy in their lives. Have not many of them grown in strength of character from the trials they endured? Souls must regain the knowledge that what they experience, both positive and negative, is providing humus for their spiritual growth. Accepting this truth will allow them to view every new circumstance that comes to them with peace and understanding.

We ask our readers to reflect deeply on what we have just said, for there is a profound truth here that must be grasped in order for the soul to progress. Every event in one's life bears with it a beautiful pearl meant to expand and elevate the soul. How can you feel fear and pain when you recognize that you can grow in strength and beauty by living through what life has to offer with dignity and grace? Keep these words in your mind and hold them close to your heart. They will bring comfort and the will to live through the trials ahead.

The great being who is the guiding soul of your planet is in the throes of a major initiation. She is raising her vibratory essence so that it can match the ascending consciousness of those who live on her surface. The turbulent energy emanating from her core is penetrating the etheric bodies of all humans, causing discordance and disruption in their energy fields. This phenomenon is contributing to the heightened anxiety, anger and animosity surfacing throughout the Earth.

Soon your planet will be irradiated with powerful vibrations that eventually will bring greater light to all life forms. For this to happen, it is necessary that Mother Earth and her inhabitants release long-held dark energy so the finer spiritual essence of light can infuse and illuminate all life on and within the planet. The intensity of painful experiences accelerates the release process, allowing for a more rapid intake of the higher vibrations. So face your tests and challenges with a serene mind and courageous heart. They are providing you the opportunity to progress up the spiral of life, moving ever closer to that ultimate reunion with your Divine Creator. It is all worth it, is it not?

# Love – The Creative Force

The light of spirit is appearing with increasing frequency all over the Earth. How can you tell that this is happening? We ask our readers to lift your heads and see with the clear eye of inner and outer knowing all that is unfolding in your world. Your times appear chaotic and frightening, but can you not discern a faint glow like the first rays of dawn as the sun rises over a dark and troubled sea? The increasing light is being projected out by many on your planet who are calling for peace and a cessation to war.

As the thought forms of unity and concern for others spread in widening circles of light-encoded love, the vibrational frequency of the Earth will start to change. The great soul that is our Mother will begin to heal when she gains respite from the violent energy emanations coming from her surface. As her heart chakra beams out a message of love and joy, more and more people will begin relating in a new way to themselves, their fellow humans and the Earth herself.

For this reason, we have stated often in this book the need for love and unity amongst the inhabitants of Earth. It forms the very core of our message to you. The single most important act an incarnating soul can perform during his or her lifetime is to increase the capacity to love. Love the Creative Force that made your life possible. Love the beautiful blue-green planet that gives you sustenance and support. Love all life existing on Earth – human, animal and plant. And finally learn to love and honor yourselves completely and without reservation.

## Learning to Love Our Enemies

The two spiritual principles that seem to be the most difficult for humans to master are learning to love themselves and their enemies. Let us consider first the people who irritate, anger or enrage you. You may ask, how can I learn to love them when I feel so negatively about them? And that is a legitimate question. Do you remember the teaching of Jesus, who told you to love your enemies? His life work was the epitome of love. He asked you to love those who have injured you, whether through word or deed. He set forth a higher standard of conduct that is not widely followed even today.

We ask you now to incorporate the teaching of "love your enemy" into the fabric of your soul. If you are able to do so, you will have taken an essential step in your spiritual growth and development. "It is a tall order," you may say. We answer, "That it is, but you can do it." The very progress of your soul depends upon it. You can start in small incremental steps. The next time a person speaks to you in a rude or offensive fashion, just know he or she has not yet learned how to express love or recognize the connection you both have at a soul level. Wish that person well and move on without registering a negative response of any kind.

As the incarnating soul moves up the ladder of difficulty in learning to love those who might be called enemies, he or she encounters people who have been hurtful to them in varying degrees of severity. These are the enemies who are difficult to love under most circumstances. It is this arena where the powerful lesson of learning to love your neighbor is found.

Hardly a soul on Earth has not been wounded by the actions of another. It is part of the human condition. But, it is how one responds that indicates his or her level of spiritual development. The old way for eons has been "an eye for an eye" or, in modern terms, "Don't get mad, get even." The practice of revenge has held sway for millennia and is still widely followed throughout the Earth today. To many, seeking retribution is automatic if they perceive that someone has injured them.

However, we would like to speak about a more spiritually advanced way of dealing with those who have hurt you. First and foremost, you must decide without wavering that you will not respond in kind. That must be a given before any other thought or action is taken. We then ask that you quiet yourself and go within, seeking the soul essence at your core. Rest in that place and offer your problem to the source of true wisdom, your higher self. Seek out that state as often as is necessary in order to find the spiritual solution to your dilemma.

As you try to determine how you will deal with the person or persons who have wounded you, you will find that revenge is not possible. Your consciousness has transcended an earlier desire to retaliate, and you now realize that the person who has hurt you is connected to you at a soul level. You know with deep conviction that you cannot reciprocate in kind if it would damage another. Once you reach that point, you have taken a major step on your soul's evolutionary journey.

Then a wide variety of options will appear as you consider an appropriate course to follow. Whatever decision you make will come from a place of spiritual awareness and will not perpetuate an ongoing negative cycle of cause and effect. You will have broken the chain of action-reaction that has been the primary method of dealing with wrongs down through the ages. You cannot even begin to imagine the amount of spiritual light that will come into your world as you treat those who have hurt you in a new and more compassionate manner.

We do not wish to imply that perpetrators should not be held accountable for their actions. If they have hurt another, they will be punished, either through the mundane laws of society or the universal Law of Cause and Effect. Even in these cases, however, true contrition and atonement will help alleviate the results of their actions. It is important to remember that most hurtful or violent words or deeds come from a state of ignorance. Only in rare instances is true malevolence involved; but when conscious enmity is present, the divine laws of the Creator always will see that justice is done. Therefore one does not need to be the final arbiter of another's hurtful actions. Is it not a relief to know that you live in a world of order and justice even though it might not be apparent at the time?

## Learning to Love Ourselves

Since love is the primary essence of the Creator, it is of utmost importance to learn how to love and honor yourself.

Loving oneself is a more rare and difficult task than you might suppose. Many forces operating within the world can negatively impact the capacity for self-love. Spouses, parents, other family members, employers, authority figures and friends can have a detrimental affect upon one's self image and esteem. Few realize today how deeply one person can harm another. Critical, disparaging words have a far more deleterious affect than is currently recognized. And if a person is physically, emotionally or sexually abused, the harm is significantly increased.

Unless an individual has a strong inner core and is able to transcend the harm being directed to him or her, a sense of unworthiness is established that adversely affects the view one has of self. Very few people are able to come from a loving and nonjudgmental place in their dealings with others. So it is that regularly and often without conscious intent, one person will do or say something that injures another. That is why we are asking our readers to take responsibility for the manner in which you treat your fellow human beings.

We are all interconnected, and each and every act or word impacts both sender and receiver. As this awareness grows, human behavior will gradually begin to change. In fact, the transition has already started. More and more incarnating souls on the Earth plane are starting to feel their energetic connection to others as well as to the very planet herself. When human beings raise their vibratory levels through acts of love and good will, the light of spirit will grow and expand all over your planet, bringing a new and more gentle day.

It is true that being treated in a caring way will help individuals feel more positively about themselves. But the real ability to love oneself can come only from within. Quiet inner attunement brought about by meditation, prayer and contemplation is the primary way to reach one's soul essence. In accessing the higher self, one bonds with the vibratory wavelength of love, which emanates from the Primal Force of Life.

One becomes aware that all life, no matter how it manifests, is a part of the Creator and therefore is imbued with the highest vibration of love. If one is created out of love, how is it possible to feel anything but love for oneself and all of life, no matter how negative the current expression might be? It is only through linking with one's soul essence that true and enduring love of self can be attained. So close your eyes, breathe deeply and go within. Only then will you know how truly beloved and loving you are.

## Functioning within a Larger Spiritual Context

The spiritual evolution of the individual soul contains a seeding process providing the stimulus for advancement. In all beings, there is a matrix that responds to anything uplifting or growth-enhancing. It is part of the genetic pattern created at the beginning of all life in this current manifestation. Everything that contains the germ of life has an inner homing device continuously pulsating in rhythm with the cosmos.

Each life form carries the impetus to keep moving towards the center of the universe in which it resides. At that center, the energy mass known as God or The Primal Being can be found. This concentration of powerful Mind has created all that lives within the boundaries of that universe. The third-dimensional brain cannot begin to comprehend the magnitude or glory of the Creator. God cannot be seen, touched or recognized in a personal, human sense. This Great Being is vibratory in nature and can be known only by a comparable energy system vibrating at the same frequency.

All contact with what seems to be a higher spiritual source is an interaction with one that has ascended and then returned to a lower vibration after mastering it. The one who is returning is an emissary from the God Force assigned to assist in the unfolding of the divine plan of creation. It is ever thus that those who are more advanced in capability help those who are on a lower level of life. The Creator established this primary assistance plan, as you humans might name it, so that all creation would have loving support and help on every step of the return journey home.

We speak of this abstract concept because now those living on your planet must know at the deepest level of their being that they are not alone and never have been. They have never been abandoned by God and have never been separated from their Source. There always has been a direct connection through all of the planes of existence to the center of their universe. This connection has been called by many different names. It is the golden cord of heaven seen by mystics of all ages. It serves as an energy conduit bringing life force to everything that lives within the universe.

All that exists is a part of the mind of the Almighty Creator. It is the intent of this Divine Force that we become true extensions of this Greater Self, and that we manifest and access all that we want and need at any given point in time. A great frequency band of information wafts through and intersects all consciousness in the many universes of creation.

Once an individual unit of consciousness can access that informational frequency band, the quality of life expands greatly. You will see all events and circumstances as incidents within a unified field, a field containing all that exists at any given time or place in the universe. When you are able to access this frequency band, you will have expanded exponentially in regards to who you are. In any given situation, you will possess a far-reaching view of all events and circumstances, providing you with a capability of galactic proportions.

# The Primal Force

The time has come for humankind to expand its idea of the Creative Power that is the life force behind every manifestation in the universe. For ages, people on your planet have thought of God in anthropomorphic terms. The concept of God has been that a spiritual being, recognizable in human form, interacts on a regular basis in their daily lives. And, in one respect, there has been some truth to this view.

God is The Primal Force underlying and activating all life. It is the vital element that existed in the beginning, alone and unknowable. This Great Force can barely be described in the limited language of the third dimension. It is electrical and vibratory in nature, possessing other qualities that cannot be stated in words. Its primary manifestation is mind force, enclosed in a sheath of love and will, that continuously desires to create.

We are aware that this description of God is far afield from the beliefs that form the norm for current spiritual and religious thought. But we bring this information to our readers to plant a new seed in the consciousness of this age. In the next one hundred years, events will occur that will greatly enlighten and expand the minds of humans on the Earth. Human awareness will grow in the recognition that Earth is connected to the galaxy and the universe in a direct and interactive way.

The knowledge base accumulated by the scientific community will be enlarged, particularly in the field of energetics. There will come a time when it will be commonly known that energy forms the basis for all life. When this occurs, the concept of God as the Primal Energy Source will become an established belief for the people of Earth. The older anthropomorphic idea of God will be seen as a necessary step in the development of the human race, but it will be replaced by a more accurate depiction – one that sees God as the generating energy force behind all that exists.

The question surely arises concerning the many personal contacts with God that individuals all over the Earth have experienced. Are they to be viewed as false? Absolutely not! Primal Mind Force has the capacity to be aware of anything occurring throughout time and space. It is able to generate the appropriate reaction through Its concentration of will and power. The personal contact souls have with God is a modulated response geared to the wavelength most suited to that entity's vibration.

So, in one way there is a connection to God. From another perspective, that link does not reflect the totality of God's energy field. Does this mean that the experience is any less valuable? On the contrary, any contact with the energy field of the Primal Force is an event of significance and has profound meaning. Each time a bonding occurs, no matter how fleeting, the soul moves upward on the spiral of life towards that final reunion with God. Can anything be more significant than this?

## Developing a More Expansive View of Life

We realize that we have been presenting a different perspective on the meaning of events that humans will experience in this twenty-first century. If one were to observe the conflict and strife without a spiritual perspective, the chaos in the world would seem intolerable. This is why we keep emphasizing the absolute necessity of developing a higher, more expansive view of life. Every incarnating soul must reconnect with the knowledge it possessed before taking on human form. Each of you knew that you would be participating in a most turbulent and chaotic period, but one that would result in humankind taking a great step upward on the spiral of life. And so you offered to participate in this momentous event, even though it would be at the cost of personal pain and suffering.

You may ask, how can I reconnect with the awareness I had before coming into this incarnation? It is so very simple. Each act of going within connects one with the spiritual core where soul wisdom resides. It is such a sweet and easy step to close one's eyes, breathe slowly and rhythmically, and slip into an altered state of consciousness, which leads to the very essence of the soul. These words describe the process of meditation where connecting with one's own soul, as well as the many realms of spirit, opens an individual to vistas and knowledge far beyond what exists on the planes of matter.

How would the twists and turns of a river look from an elevated view, far above the course of the river's flow? You would be able to observe the source of the river as well as its point of termination. The river, with its many changes in direction, leads to an eventual end not yet seen by those standing anywhere along its course. Humans who have not expanded their spiritual viewing do not have the advantage of knowing what their spiritual goal is or how their current lifetime is a part of their soul's journey.

This is why we continue to urge you to expand your inner knowing through meditation. It is a direct conduit to the Creator of All That Is. This practice fine-tunes and upgrades your nervous system, which serves as the electrical wiring for your human body. It pulls more highly refined vibratory energies into your physical form, strengthening your blood, bones, organs and glands, and increasing physical vitality and longevity. Meditation also expands intuition and extrasensory awareness, two very necessary abilities for the next step in human growth and development. With all of these great advantages and gifts, why would you not make meditation a daily practice of high priority?

Now we bring this second book of writings to an end. We have covered a wide variety of topics, many that will expand the minds and hearts of those who read our message. Our words carry an energetic imprint that will open pathways to the brain and accelerate the process of human evolutionary development for our readers. It is time for those of you who live on the Earth plane to raise your heads, open your eyes and awaken to the reality of who you truly are in the divine scheme of things!

You are travelers on a holy journey of reunion with the Divine Source that created you. You are meant to encounter every kind of experience necessary for soul growth and development. When you have done so, you will reunite with the God Source as a beloved child of the Almighty. Is the journey not well worth the pain that appears in your lives?

We ask that you hold the understanding and wisdom you have gained in your hearts as you move through your current lives on Earth. Extend your hands in love and respect to your fellow humans and all the creatures in your world. Remember that you are all One and interconnected at a soul level. Live knowing that this link also extends throughout time and space, uniting you with your Creator in a direct and ongoing partnership. Learn to feel the love and support coming to you in every moment of your life and beyond.

We urge you to live with courage and grace through the coming years as a new Heaven and a new Earth emerge from the dissolution of your Old World. You can make a far better one, if you have the courage of heart and strength of spirit to stay the course.

Help eradicate the ills of the Old World, which have enslaved the inhabitants of your planet for eons. Rise up the spiral of life and join those on the realm of spirit who are waiting to embrace you. Can you not feel their love being beamed to you on waves of shimmering light? They are reminding you, "We are all One dancing in the fields of the Holy Spirit to reach the Highest Good."

This ends our second series of transmissions.

We love you all.

The Lightbringers

# Definition of Terms

**Chakras:** Rotating circles or conduits that bring life force called *prana* into the physical body through the endocrine glands. They are located just outside the body in an energetic sheath surrounding the physical form. Most people living on the Earth plane are unable to see them at this point in human development.

**Duality:** The underlying theme of the universe that offers two principles for expression, often times opposing in nature. The Divine Creator establishes a primary idea for any given universe. In Earth's universe, duality is the basic framework for all life. Every dynamic contains the interaction of opposites, out of which eventually comes the realization that only unity can bring peace and fulfillment to the soul.

**Etheric Body:** A vibrational energy form surrounding the human body. It is oval in shape and located approximately four inches away from the physical body. It supplies energy or life force and mirrors to some degree the characteristics of the physical body. Occasionally, those with heightened sensory abilities can see it.

**Forcefield:** A space containing energy surrounding anything that exists. All life, whether it is physical, emotional, mental or spiritual, has its own energetic field. While not recognized at this time, every interaction, at a primary level, is a commingling of different energy fields. Once this principle is understood, humanity will take a major step upward in its spiritual growth and development.

**Gaia:** A name for the Earth. Humans used it extensively as a term of endearment in earlier times. It is feminine in nature and, when spoken, contains an energetic vibration that replicates the soul essence of the planet.

**Group Soul:** A joining of individual souls within a larger spiritual framework for a specific purpose on behalf of God's Divine Plan. All that exists within the realms of spirit and matter lives within an ever-greater sphere of influence — just as the Earth is found in a solar system within a galaxy located in a larger universal scheme.

**Initiation:** An agonizing experience where suffering and pain cause the death of an old pattern of behavior, which is replaced by a more elevated state of awareness. On the human level, the initiatory process can occur through loss, death, sickness, betrayal, and abandonment, to name a few.

**Law of Cause and Effect:** A principle that operates with undeviating force towards all life throughout the universe. Its basic purpose is to maintain balance, equilibrium and harmony in the worlds of the Creative Force. This Law fulfills its purpose by guaranteeing that for every act or cause, no matter how small or insignificant, there will be an accompanying response at some point in time.

**Law of Manifestation:** A basic principle operating in the world of matter that provides the framework within which physical creation occurs. Anything brought into being at the third dimensional level does so within the context of the Law of Manifestation. The process begins at the level of mental causation or idea. It then moves to the emotional level of desire, which combines energy and commitment, and finally enters the realm of physical reality where the actual work occurs. In the future, humans will be able to manifest physically by just envisioning what they want to create, and it will come into being through the power of their mind force.

**Matrix:** The womb from which something originates. All life comes forth from an original source that places its imprint on the emerging form. This creative principle holds true at every dimensional level in the universe.

**Paradigm:** An energetic model within which a particular pattern of life operates. This construct imprints at all levels those individuals who agree with its basic premises. It provides a rationale for living by setting forth an example for humans to follow. However, when a different stimulus shifts the mental belief system, the paradigm is discarded for a new one that more accurately reflects the change in consciousness.

**Universal Frequency Band of Information:** A vast reservoir of information on any subject that humans may need or want. It exists on the realm of spirit and contains all knowledge accumulated through time. The computer Internet of today is a faint replica of this spiritual phenomenon. When the people of Earth become able to access it, they will take an evolutionary step forward of great magnitude.

**Vibration:** The background of energy found throughout the universe. It can best be described as a rapid movement back and forth, similar to a pendulum. It emanates out of the Mind of the Creator. Its primary essence is rhythmic motion, which provides the necessary force for every act of creation.

**Vortex:** A mass of whirling energy containing a center of complete calm from which the circular movement emerges. At the physical level, a hurricane or whirlpool best exemplifies its primary characteristics. This circulating energy mass possesses a magnetic power that draws in anything caught by its motion. In the future, humans will learn how to harness powerful vortex forces and use them in a wide variety of ways.

# INDEX

## A

Aboriginal cultures, 49-50, 85-86
Alchemical change, 30
Almighty Creator, 155
Americas, the, 124
Anthropomorphic idea of God, 157
Apostles, 92
Armageddon, 136
Ascension, 96-97, 99, 137
Astral body, 97
Astral travel, 10
Astronomical observatories, 35
Atlantis, 15
Auras, 77
Australia, 85

## B

Blueprint, 35, 49, 59-60, 67, 107, 109, 127-130, 136, 138
Brain, 16, 86-88, 91, 97, 99, 102-103, 105, 110-111, 131, 133-134, 154, 159
Buddha, 107

## C

Canada, 46, 128
Caribbean, 136
Chakra, 93, 150, 162
Children of God, 132, 143
Christianity, 70
Co-creators, 14, 17, 88, 114, 132
Collective energy field, 7
Confucius, 107
Consciousness, 1-3, 6-7, 9-10, 14, 18, 22-24, 28, 32, 39-40, 45, 53, 60-67, 69-71, 76-77, 79-81, 87-88, 95, 99-100, 102, 104, 106, 108, 111-112, 114,116
Constitution of the United States, 46, 52

Creative Force, 19, 28, 51, 55, 67, 72, 80, 91, 107, 141, 150, 163
Creative Idea, 85
Creator of All That Is, 6, 10, 71, 89, 125, 158
Crusades of the Middle Ages, 66
Cycles, 9, 16, 43, 45-46, 138

## D

Dawn of time, 65
Death, 1, 5, 21, 23, 31, 43-44, 49-50, 62, 65, 69, 126, 132, 145,163
Dimension, 10, 17, 40-41, 46, 65, 73, 84, 86, 89-91, 95-98, 100, 102-103, 105, 107-113, 115, 131, 133
Divine Creator, 2, 10, 19, 31, 54-57, 60, 95, 98, 113, 143, 147, 162
Divine Dance of Life, 109
Divine Oneness, 14, 37, 86, 88, 104, 113
Divine Order, 33, 45, 57, 71, 119, 140
Divine Source, 9, 22, 159
Divine Wisdom, 108
DNA, 14, 61, 86, 88, 102, 122
*Dreaming a New World*, 1-3, 5, 32, 139
Duality, 6, 9, 19, 31, 53, 58, 64, 66, 72-75, 77-78, 81-82, 137, 162

## E

Earth, 3, 5-10, 13-41, 43, 46-48, 54-58, 60-74, 77
Earth changes, 30, 129, 137, 139
Earth Mother, 23
Earth plane, 6, 18, 20, 39-40, 54-58, 61, 65, 67, 71-72, 74, 77, 83, 86, 93, 98, 100, 106, 109-110, 113, 121, 153,159, 162

Earth's astral plane, 27
Earth's crust, 138-139
Earth's vibratory atmosphere, 29
Electrical vibratory waves, 93
Electromagnetic forcefield, 17
Endocrine glands, 97, 123, 162
Energetics, 156
Energy field, 7-8, 36, 91, 93, 95-96,
    106, 114, 116, 146, 157, 162
Etheric body, 93, 162
Etheric plane, 103
Europe, 47
Extrasensory awareness, 105-106, 159

**F**

Fertile Crescent, 64, 70
Forcefield, 8, 17, 32, 37, 40, 43, 60,
    70, 75-76, 84, 89, 93-94, 162
Four Primary Forces, 122
Fourth Dimension, 2, 10, 83, 90-92,
    99, 100, 111, 117
Fourth-Dimensional travel, 92, 95
Fourth-Dimensional reality, 99

**G**

Gaia, 23, 34, 37-39, 162
Gateways to higher dimensions, 65
God as the Generating Energy
    Force, 157
God Force, 77, 95, 101, 109, 113,
    131-132, 155
Godhead, 54-55, 81, 138
Golden Age on Earth, 56
Great Awakening, 6, 27, 120
Great Britain, 67
Great Mother That Sustains
    All Life, 25
Great Purification, 124
Great Spirit, 22, 38-39
Greater Self, 155
Greeks, 145

Group soul, ix, 1, 6, 63, 163
Guardians of the Flame, 85-86
Guide, 92, 97, 99

**H**

High-density laboratories, 84
Higher Power, 54, 122
Higher realms, 10, 19, 65, 89, 96-97,
    104-105, 107, 109, 112, 132-133
Holy Spirit, 160
Human beings, 5, 10, 15-17, 24-25,
    29, 35-38, 43, 45, 49, 54, 65, 70-
    71, 78, 84, 88-89, 103, 105, 107,
    110-111, 114-116, 122-123, 129,
    135, 153
Human race, 16, 37, 56, 58, 69, 78-
    80, 82, 87, 121-122, 157
Humanity, 6-7, 14, 23-24, 27, 31, 33,
    37, 39, 60-61, 82, 103, 105-106,
    109-110, 115-116, 126-128, 131,
    135-137

**I**

Idea of the Whole, 44
Incarnating souls, 9-10, 28, 38, 56-
    57, 71, 112, 116, 125-126, 128,
    130, 139, 141, 144, 153
Incarnation, 27, 29, 78, 106, 124,
    142, 158
Indigenous people, 17, 37, 104
Informational frequency band, 155
Initiation, 9, 22-26, 31-32, 38, 61-64,
    66, 68, 71, 142, 146, 163
Intent, 20, 44, 48-50, 59, 76-77, 91-
    92, 95, 98, 106, 109, 113, 128,
    137-139, 153, 155
Interdimensional travel, 97-98, 105,
    112, 116, 121
Iraq, 62-64, 66-70, 74, 76, 81-82
Iraqi people, 62-64, 67
Islam, 70

## J
Japan, 47
Jesus the Christ, 40
Judaism, 70

## L
Law of Duality, 19, 64-66, 78
Law of Love, 47, 81
Law of Manifestation, 58-60, 163
Lemuria, 15
Life Force of the Almighty, 85
Lightbringers, 2, 7, 107, 160
Long Count, 36
Love, 2, 5, 9-10, 17-19, 24, 28-33, 37, 39, 47, 55, 57, 60-62, 64, 70, 73, 76-79, 81, 107, 120, 126, 130, 132-133, 138, 140, 143, 145, 149-154, 156, 159-160

## M
Mary, 92
Matrix, 6, 14, 21-22, 13, 45-48, 60, 64, 66, 70, 77-78, 84, 98, 108, 120, 129, 135, 138, 154, 164
Maya, 36
Meditation, 1, 17, 27-28, 40, 76-77, 94, 98, 112-113, 123, 143, 153, 158-159
Mexico, 46
Middle East, 54, 69
Milky Way Galaxy, 7, 104, 134
Millennium, 9, 22, 58, 105, 121, 129-131
Miracles, 79
Moon, 45, 51
Mother Earth, 31-32, 37-38, 70, 129-130, 137-138, 140, 142-143, 145-146
Multidimensional travelers, 131
Muslim World, 74

## N
Native American, 92
Natural disasters, 30-33, 38, 136-137
Nature of Reality, 5
New Age, 21-22, 14, 19, 78, 121-122
New Earth, 6, 20, 24, 39, 41, 57, 80, 82, 127, 140, 159
New Heaven, 20, 39, 41, 57, 61, 80, 127, 140, 159
New human species, 6, 10, 70, 87, 138
New prototype of human being, 11, 134
New World, 61, 124, 126, 139-140
New World view, 61
Non-Earth beings, 133
North American continent, 128
Now, the, 83, 90-91, 111

## O
Old World, 21, 60, 125, 140, 145, 159, 160
Oneness, 14, 37, 75-76, 78, 86, 88, 104, 113

## P
Pacific Ocean, 46
Paradigm, 61, 116, 124-125, 128, 164
Pathway to higher realms, 89
Plan of the Almighty, 58
Plan of the Creator, 6, 34, 45, 71, 110, 137
Polarity, 10, 64, 72-74, 77, 138
Portals, 65
Prayer, 1, 19, 28, 32, 40, 76-77, 94, 98, 112, 123, 143, 153
Primal Being, 154
Primal Force, 141, 154, 156-157
Pythagoras, 107

**Q**

Quantum leap forward, 22
Quantum physics, 115
Quantum theory, 115

**R**

Realm of spirit, 1-3, 5-6, 18-20, 33,
    39-40, 53-54, 61, 69, 85, 94, 106,
    108, 123, 135, 143, 160, 164
Rebirth, 21, 16, 31, 43, 145
Rhythmic breathing, 19, 99

**S**

Saints, 92
Second World War, 47
Sexuality, 5, 28
Shamans, 96, 104-105
Sixth sense, 87
Sleeplessness,20
Socrates, 107
Soul Essence, 34-35, 37, 39, 73, 91,
    112, 124, 151, 162
Soul essence of Gaia, 37
Soul journeys, 10
Soul's data bank, 84
Soul's memory bank, 85
Source of All That Is, 111
Spiral of life, 21, 23-24, 38-39, 54,
    60, 62, 65, 67, 70, 72, 78, 82, 85,
    88, 115, 120, 122, 124, 127-128,
    135, 138, 147, 157-158, 160
Spiritual weather map, 136
Spiritualization of matter, 120
Star maps, 36
Star people, 135
Subconscious data banks, 15
Subconscious mind, 15-16, 26
Summer of 2004, 81, 135

**T**

Third Dimension, 10, 84-85, 89-91,
    94-95, 99, 108, 110-112, 156, 163
Third World War, 54, 56
Transformation, 6-7, 17, 20-21, 23-
    24, 28, 39, 58, 60, 88, 98, 105,
    134, 143
Triune reality, 108
Tsunami, 30
Twentieth century, 26-27, 47, 56, 58
Twenty-first century, 10-11, 22, 24,
    54, 56, 58, 81, 110, 112, 119,
    121, 124, 129-131, 157

**U**

UFOs, 135
Ultimate Source of Energy, 109
Unified field, 41, 157
United Nations, 60
United States, 45-52, 64-68, 74, 76,
    81, 124, 128, 133
Unity, 9, 53, 59, 72-73, 75-78, 81,
    135, 137, 149-150, 162
Universal Law, 47, 64, 81
Universal Law of Cause and
    Effect, 54, 67, 152
Universal Mind, 53, 84

**V**

Vibration/vibrational, 1-2, 8, 23-24,
    27, 34, 39-40, 43-44, 55-57, 65,
    67, 70, 77, 83, 87, 90-91, 93, 95,
    98-99, 102, 106, 113, 120, 138,
    146, 149, 154, 158, 162, 164
Vibratory field, 24, 27, 33, 65, 117
Vibratory frequencies, 7, 31
Vibratory light, 20
Vibratory rate, 59, 89-90, 98
Vibratory wavelength, 17, 154
Visualization, 76-77

Vortex, 64-65, 75, 85, 90-91, 93, 140, 142, 164

## W
War on terrorism, 74
Will of the Divine Creator, 54
Womb of the Mother, 144
World Wars, 47

## Y
Yoga, 97

## Z
Zenith, 44, 47